D1016972

Joy is the serious business of heaven.

— C. S. LEWIS

The Navigators is an international Christian organization. Our mission is to reach, disciple, and equip people to know Christ and to make Him known through successive generations. We envision multitudes of diverse people in the United States and every other nation who have a passionate love for Christ, live a lifestyle of sharing Christ's love, and multiply spiritual laborers among those without Christ.

NavPress is the publishing ministry of The Navigators. NavPress publications help believers learn biblical truth and apply what they learn to their lives and ministries. Our mission is to stimulate spiritual formation among our readers.

Library of Congress Catalog Card Number: 98-22233
ISBN 1-57683-098-5
Cover illustration by E. Chadwick/Woodriver Media Inc.

Some of the anecdotal illustrations in this book are true to life and are included with the permission of the persons involved. All other illustrations are either composites of real situations or fictitious, and any resemblance to people living or dead is coincidental.

Unless otherwise identified, all Scripture in this publication is from the *HOLY BIBLE: NEW INTERNATIONAL VERSION* (NIV©). Copyright © 1973, 1978, 1984, International Bible Society. Used by permission of Zondervan Bible Publishers. Used by permission. The other version used is *The Message* (MSG). Copyright ©1993 Eugene Peterson. Used by permission from NavPress.

MacDonald, Hope.
      Letters from heaven / Hope MacDonald.
         p.   cm.
      Includes bibliographical references.
      ISBN 1-57683-098-5
      1. Heaven—Christianity.   I. Title.
BT846.2.M325 1998   98-22233
236' .24—dc21   CIP

Printed in the United States of America

1 2 3 4 5 6 7 8 9 10 11 12 13 14 / 05 04 03 02 01 00 99 98

LETTERS FROM
Heaven

FOREWORD BY J.I.PACKER

Hope MacDonald

NAVPRESS ◖
BRINGING TRUTH TO LIFE
NavPress Publishing Group
P.O. Box 35001, Colorado Springs, Colorado 80935

LETTERS FROM
Heaven

To
my beloved husband

Harry MacDonald

for blessing my life on earth
with a "little bit of heaven."

Books by the same author:

Discovering How to Pray
Discovering the Joy of Obedience
When Angels Appear
Traditional Values for Today's New Woman

Contents

Acknowledgments

I would like to express my thanks to the following friends who prayed faithfully for me each day during the writing of this book.

Patti Bylsma	Beverly Miller
Mary Kay Cowan	Dianne Morton
Dorene Craig	Linda Peritore
Zelma Doig	Jane Short
Shirley Gilmore	Jean Spitzer
Doris Johnson	Patty Taylor
Jan Lentz	Judy Wackerbarth
Marilyn Mead	

I also want to thank my editor, Terri Hibbard, for her thoughtful insights.

Foreword

HOPE MACDONALD would like to see today's Christians thinking more about heaven. So would I. The stronger our hope of glory and the livelier our devotion, the better our all-around spiritual health.

But how are we to think of heaven? Well, our brains have two lobes. The left lobe is for logic (definitions, analyses, arguments) while the right lobe is for imagination (stories, drama, art, empathy). All real thought about life's realities, and certainly about any aspects of God and godliness, involves both logic and imagination, as every book of the Bible clearly shows. So thinking about heaven means blending these brainpowers to envisage perfect sin-free goodness and pain-free happiness in a perfected love-relationship with the Father, Son, and Holy Spirit, and the angels and saints. Indeed from this perspective we gain, not a preview of heaven (which we can only picture in terms of the life we know, minimally adjusted), but a sense of heaven's quality—the sort of life and joy that awaits those who belong to Jesus Christ.

Children love to chew candy because of its sweetness. In the same way, once the awareness of heaven's glory has become clear, the children of God will chew it mentally over and over again, finding in it both sweetness and strength for their hearts.

Hope MacDonald understands this and writes accordingly. She projects heaven's beauty and delight in a way that will leave readers refreshed and grateful. Read on—you will soon see what I mean.

J. I. PACKER
Professor of Systematic Theology at Regent College in Vancouver, B.C.
Author of *Knowing God* and many other books and articles

Preface

*"Whenever I see the beauty of God's earth,
I rejoice to imagine the beauty of His heaven."*

These words, seen on a poster long ago, remain the inspiration behind this book. *Letters From Heaven* is a joy-filled book about the quality of life awaiting us in heaven. It's a book built on the foundation of God's unchanging truth.

The letters and both of the characters are fictional. There is no way any person on earth can go to his or her mailbox and find a letter from heaven in it. Nor is there any way to write a letter to someone in heaven, go to the post office, buy a "celestial stamp," and expect it to be delivered to the "Gates of Pearl." How these letters go back and forth between heaven and earth is left to the imagination.

My prayer for each reader is that you will catch a glimpse of the incredible glory God has waiting for all who put their trust in Him and be challenged to live each day on earth with heaven in view.

HOPE MACDONALD
Seattle, Washington

Introduction

Have you ever looked up at the sky and wondered about heaven? I have. It was a cold, blustery afternoon, and I was driving home from the funeral for a friend's son. My heart was as heavy as the dark clouds that hung in the Seattle sky. *Why did seventeen-year-old Jeremy have to die before his dreams and talents had a chance to be realized?*

Where is he now? I wondered. Oh, I knew he was in heaven, *but how did he get there so quickly? And what is he going to* do *there? And why is he in heaven? What did he do to get there? How will his parents go on living without his captivating smile and intense blue eyes?*

As I wrestled with these questions, I gazed upward again and saw it. A radiant double rainbow suddenly appeared in the darkened sky. With the rainbow a quiet peace of absolute assurance filled my heart. Jeremy was with Jesus. At that moment. In heaven.

And someday he will meet his mother and father at the gate of heaven and welcome them home. Maybe he will take his fun-loving brothers, Joshua and Joel, on a sightseeing tour. They will join him in running a race, jumping hurdles, hitting home runs, or flying down a ski slope of fresh powder. He'll welcome his family and friends who wept over his untimely death. He'll greet with special joy those classmates who received Jesus Christ as Savior at his funeral. What reunions those will be!

That night I woke up still thinking about Jeremy. I told the Lord how I wished I had gone to see him the week before he died because I wanted to share some thoughts with him about heaven. Then the idea occurred to me, *Why not put those thoughts in a book and call it* Letters From Heaven?

After three years of research, the time came to sit down and write the book. During those years my friends often asked how I could write a book about a subject they felt could be summed up in a few pages. To be honest, I felt much the same way. I wondered how I could write about a place I'd never seen. I remembered that rule number one in good writing is to know your subject well by reading and studying what has already been written about it. In the midst of all my reading I found a helpful statement by Peter Kreeft. He said a book is conceived out of the writings of many centuries gone by. Good writing is "piggyback thinking; you stand on my shoulders, I stand on Lewis', Lewis stands on [George] MacDonald's, MacDonald stands on Augustine's, Augustine stands on Saint Paul's, Saint Paul stands on Christ's. That far up, you see far. We need a Great Chain of Thinking to see the Great Chain of Being. Here is one small link."[1]

And so I gathered up my notebook and began to search the bookstores and libraries for books about heaven. Although I found many good books on the subject written during the twentieth century, it didn't take me long to discover that the books I enjoyed most were written centuries ago by monks and saints of old: Saint Thomas Aquinas, Saint Augustine, Saint Bernard of Clairvaux, and John Bunyan. Heaven was very real to them, and they had much to say about it.

In spite of the fact that a recent poll in *Newsweek* stated that 75 percent of all Americans plan on going to heaven, I learned from conversations with people that they really knew very little about heaven. Without the loss of a loved one or a walk through the valley of suffering, we prefer not to think about heaven just yet. We're a lot like Scarlett O'Hara, in *Gone with the Wind,* who was fond of saying, "I'll think about it tomorrow." We all plan on going there—but not today. We're more apt to want to go to Hawaii first!

Why do we feel this way? Is it because we have such a distorted concept of heaven? Do we actually think we're going to sit on a cloud and play a harp forever? Will we really stand around the throne of God and sing hosannas to Him for eternity? And would God, our great Creator-Redeemer, even want to sit and listen to our endless singing?

Maybe the real reason we put off thinking about heaven is because we dread death. It's more comfortable not to think of our own mortality. The fear of being separated from everyone we love and everything we've ever known is more than most of us can bear. But these negative fears can play an important, positive role in our lives. They can send us on a pursuit of truth—God's truth—that brings freedom from fear. English historian Paul Johnson said, "The fear of the unknown is the beginning of belief."[2] When we begin to face these haunting fears, which plague all of us at times, and discover the reason behind them, we often find they can be transformed into belief—belief in God and the promises of heaven found in His Word. That's what this book is all about.

Points to Ponder

In dealing with the subject of heaven, we must answer this basic question: *Is there life after death, or is heaven merely a leftover superstition from the murky Dark Ages or a creation of humankind's own wishful thinking?* Kreeft says heaven is "either a fascinating lie or a fascinating fact."[3] There is only one source for finding the truth about heaven—the Bible. It's our guidebook to life. It tells us where we've been in history, where we are in the present, and where we'll be in eternity. In it God has given us all the knowledge about heaven our human minds are capable of understanding while here on earth. It may not be exhaustive knowledge, but it is God's true knowledge.

Where does life after death take place? The Bible says that for the believer, it takes place in heaven, where Jesus is. To understand something about heaven we must first consider the question, *Who is Jesus?* According to the Scriptures, Jesus is God incarnate. Author Joni Eareckson Tada says that Jesus is "God wearing a human face."[4] He lived for thirty-three years on this planet, in space, time, and history. He showed us, through example, that God is love. He died on the cross to reconcile a lost world to Himself. On the third day He arose bodily from the grave. He conquered our two great enemies—sin and death—for all eternity. After His resurrection, He appeared for forty days to His disciples and to groups of up to five hundred people. He then ascended into heaven, His eternal home, the place He has prepared for each person who receives Him as Savior and Lord.[5]

The Use of Symbols

We may have shrouded heaven in great mystery today, but Scripture has not. It is mentioned over five hundred times from Genesis to Revelation. Heaven is God's world. In Matthew 25:34 Jesus tells us it is the perfect "kingdom prepared for you since the creation of the world." There is so much we can know and understand about heaven. While the Bible gives us some specific truths that leave no room for speculation or doubt, it often uses symbols that help us identify with the glory that awaits God's people in heaven. Symbols are a representation of something else. A wedding ring is a symbol of lasting love. A lion is often used as a symbol of courage. When the Bible refers to streets of gold in heaven, this image is a symbol of the great beauty and wealth of heaven. On earth, gold often symbolizes the importance or value we place on money. In heaven, gold is something we'll walk on.

A cross represents the finished work of Christ. The empty cross is a symbol of His death and resurrection. Many great hymns are filled with symbols that represent the believer's deep love and worship of God. Author and lecturer C. S. Lewis said, "All the scriptural imagery (harps, crowns, gold, etc.) is, of course, a merely symbolical attempt to express the inexpressible. . . . People who take these symbols literally might as well think that when Christ told us to be like doves, he meant that we were to lay eggs."[6]

The Use of Parables

When Jesus lived on earth, He often taught in parables. A parable is nothing more than a little story that teaches a big truth.

Jesus used simple stories of a seed, a coin, a prodigal son, a lost sheep, and many other things to bring out divine truths. His parables are laced with hidden treasures of knowledge.

In writing this book, I too rely on symbols and parables to give us a glimpse into heaven's glory. I rely on human language to describe the utterly indescribable. I use natural words to illustrate the supernatural. Paul faced this same problem in attempting to portray heaven as simply having to use inexpressible words. And even though I may have needed to use my "sanctified imagination" at times in these letters, I built them on objective biblical truth. The parables and symbols are simply meant to help us think about the *quality* of life in heaven in terms we can comprehend. It's so easy to get caught up in the mystical, nebulous concepts of heaven that all true understanding of it disappears. Think how God had to reach when describing the glories of heaven in earthly language. That could have been even more challenging than creating the world!

True Knowledge Begins with Wonder

Have you ever wondered where heaven is? What it's like? How to get there? Did you ever wonder what you'll be like once you are there? What you will do? Will your choices today really affect your eternal destiny? What part does heaven play in the way you live on earth? There are so many questions to think about. Did you ever wonder what it would be like to sit down with a loved one who is already there and have a good long talk? I have. I wonder what Jeremy would say to us from the other side. How much easier it would be if we could hear the responses of those already in heaven.

I am learning that wonder is a good thing. Theologian Dr. Marty Folsom says, "True knowledge begins with wonder."[7] *Letters From Heaven* was written when I began to think about these questions. This pondering led me on a quest for answers. The result is this book, which I pray will be a source of truth, comfort, and joy to each reader.

And now as you turn to the letters, let the apostle John set your imagination soaring above the clouds with his words of wonder:

"Then I looked and oh!—a door open into Heaven!"[8]

CHAPTER ONE

Is Heaven a Place?

Dear Child of God,

Today, as always, is a day of matchless perfection in heaven. The crystal air is fragrant with the scent of flowers. Everything is drenched in beauty. With a book tucked under my arm I hummed a song of praise as I strolled down the wandering pathway, past emerald green lawns and my neighbors' gardens, and out into the countryside. I looked forward with joyful anticipation to my reading and meditation time.

No sooner had I settled down under the leafy branches of my favorite tree, when an angel dressed in sunshine approached me. This heavenly messenger told me of a new and exciting opportunity that had been given to me. And it has to do with you!

You see, God cares about the many situations you're facing right now. He knows you've just received word of your father's terminal illness. God understands your deep love for your father; how he was always a model of what God intended fathers to be; how, as a child, you shared a close, special relationship; and how you've remained in his heart and he in yours.

Along with coming to grips with the mortality of a loved one for the first time, you're also facing the new role passed on to you as the only child. You, the cared-for child, now find yourself the emotional supporter and caregiver for your parents. That's a major transition. Because you love your parents, it's not a hardship, but it's not always easy.

And then there's your own active family to care for. Your son is completing his first year of college, your daughter will soon be a senior in high school, and your eight-year-old twins keep the entire family going in different directions at the same time!

In addition to your new role as your parents' parent and the daily care of your family, there's the new job offer—an opportunity to join a prestigious law firm across the country. Ordinarily, this wouldn't be a problem. You've moved many times during your marriage. When the older children were young, you even lived in Brazil. But times have changed and so have the needs of your family. Even though your children are older, in many ways they need you more now than before.

So you feel torn in too many directions. Last night you cried out, "Oh, Lord! You know everything I'm dealing with right now. It hurts so much. I'm so confused. I don't know which way to go. I know you care about my pain as well as the suffering and loss my parents are experiencing. I know you care about my children and our family's excitement over this possible promotion and all the work that has led up to it. I need You now. I need Your love. I need Your comfort and direction and wisdom. I wish I could have just a glimpse of You. Are You really there? If You are, please help me!"

God heard your prayer, and it touched His heart. As a demonstration of His promised comfort, strength, and guidance in the days ahead, He has entrusted me with the joyful privilege of writing a series of letters to you from heaven. I'm absolutely certain that once you get a glimpse of the glory of heaven, you'll also get a new perspective on life. It's true that your outward circumstances may not change much, but inwardly you'll receive a deep sense of peace and a new understanding of God's love. You'll find new courage and power to meet every situation you face.

I'm looking forward to my time of sharing with you through these letters. Frankly, I can't think of anything I'd rather be involved in. I consider this to be an opportunity full of joy. How do I explain the glories of heaven in earthly language? I'm sure it will take all of my God-given creativity. I'll try to focus each letter on one subject. I must confess it will take discipline not to say everything at once!

The prospect of sharing heaven with you makes me feel like a child anticipating Christmas. I can see I must be careful or these letters could easily become a book!

Yours from the Other Side

&

Dear Child of God,
I'm sitting on my porch with a tall glass of Heaven's Iced Tea. It makes me happy to think someday you'll enjoy this drink with me. By the way, I was glad to hear my first letter was an encouragement to you. I know when I went through difficult times, it helped to know someone cared. Of course we both

know your heavenly Father is aware of every detail of your life and cares tremendously when you are hurting.

I was also happy to hear you've felt God's love and comfort in a new way recently. I sensed your relief when you mentioned the decision not to move the family at this time. The peace you felt once the decision was made was God's gentle confirmation to you.

I've been giving a lot of thought to where I should start these letters. I guess the beginning would be best! I like the way the Bible begins with such precise words of authority, "In the beginning, God created the heavens and the earth."[1] Just as the earthly world is a specially created place, so is heaven. It's God's home. It's where all of His angels live. It's also the place where your loved ones, who have walked across the valley of death by way of the Cross, are now living. Heaven is being home at last—with Jesus!

Since you asked about what you'll find in heaven, I thought I'd share with you some of its basic features. One truth that stands out above all others is that heaven is a place where God's perfect will is always accomplished. I had to smile when I wrote the word "place" because it means a specific, definite location. There's nothing vague or mysterious about the reality that heaven exists as a real location—even though from your side it seems a great mystery. Remember the words of Jesus: "I am going there to prepare a place for you. . . . I will come back and take you to be with me that you also may be where I am."[2] There certainly isn't any room for doubt in that statement. Neither is there any doubt about the fact that heaven is a place of new beginnings, new purpose, new relationships, and a new home. It's also a place of perfect safety. That's something people on earth know very little about.

You see, heaven is a very specific place. It's just like Switzerland, China, or your country. However, you can't run down to your local travel office and get a map with directions on how to find it. There are no charts neatly laid out with the best route outlined in red. But God has given you something far more valuable than a torn and tattered map to Treasure Island. He's given you the Bible. It comes with a specific map and definite directions to heaven. These directions are clearly outlined in red—with the blood of Jesus Christ pointing the way.

The one key to remember is that you must make an advanced reservation. It's like when you plan a vacation. You decide on the destination and study brochures and guidebooks to choose where you'd like to stay. Then you call ahead or send in a check to reserve your room or suite. You're given a confirmation number and a receipt stating you have a guaranteed reservation. Well, that's similar to how you make your plans to go to heaven. You read and study your Bible where you discover God's invitation of eternal life in heaven. Then you decide you want to spend eternity there, so you follow God's instructions by receiving Jesus Christ as Savior and Lord. (We'll go into more detail on this in a later letter.) Your name is instantly recorded in the Book of Life at that time. From then on you hold a guaranteed reservation in heaven (even though you don't know your departure date!). And God's Holy Word is your receipt.

The Bible often refers to heaven as a city whose builder and ruler is God. Can you imagine what a place designed by God is like, a place free from all sin and death? In the Bible it's called New Jerusalem, the capital city of heaven. Sometimes it's referred to as the Holy City. Built on a foundation of precious stones, the light of God shines like jasper on gates made of pearl. These gates are always open so all of heaven's citizens may come and go as they please. The city is lit by God's radiance so there's no need for the sun.[3] Filled with celestial music, continual praises to God, and infectious joy and laughter, it's where everyone and everything lives in complete harmony with God. Can you imagine it? Maybe it would help if you could imagine New York, London, or Paris being a city where everyone gets along and serves God. Now wouldn't that be something to experience!

Knowing that I would be describing some of the basic wonders of heaven today, I decided to walk over to the beautiful River of Life spoken of in the book of Revelation. How I wish you could have come with me. With pen and paper in hand, I sat down on the river bank. Drifts of flowers surrounded me and a quiet stillness filled the warm air. The crystal water, blue as sapphire, flowed from the very throne of God.

Tall trees line both sides of the river. Winding paths lead through the luxurious gardens. Fields, embroidered with bright flowers, stretch out as far as you can see. Benches are scattered along the way where you can sit and enjoy the quiet beauty of God's creation. Often little lambs, whiter than new-fallen snow, leap among the flowers. I could hear the quiet murmur of the bees and see the flashing colors of God's light on the wings of the singing birds. In the midst of all this splendor stands the stately Tree of Life, clothed in dignity and grandeur and watered by the River of Life. It produces twelve golden fruits whose leaves bring healing to all nations.[4]

I couldn't help thinking of Jesus when He encountered the woman at the well that day in Samaria and offered her a drink of Living Water.[5] Here in heaven we can drink of that Living Water from the River of Life at any time. Can you imagine never thirsting again? In heaven all of our needs and longings are satisfied.

There's so much more I can tell you about this wonderful place. But I will save it for other letters so you can have time to think about what I've already written.

Yours from the Other Side

P.S. I look forward to responding to your thoughts and questions as we go along.

❧

Dear Child of God,
Thanks for your letter. Your question about the mansion Jesus is preparing for you is a good one. It reminded me of thoughts I had before I arrived here. I remember singing songs about my mansion in heaven and feeling like I really didn't want it. I pictured myself alone in this big rambling building, and it always seemed rather cold and lonely to think about. It's so easy to have misperceptions about something we haven't experienced.

To help you with your own concerns, I thought you might like to know about the kind of house I live in. First of all, let me remind you that your home won't necessarily be like mine. (No tract houses in heaven!) God is preparing a place for you with everything He knows you will enjoy. You may choose who you want to live with or decide to live alone. That's something God leaves up to you.

To reach my home you go down a tree-lined country road, past gardens filled with flowers more fragrant than any earthly ones you know. Sweeping green lawns lead to comfortable estates settled far back from the golden pathway. As you near my home, you hear happy voices coming from my neighbor's porch. Since my neighborhood has many picturesque gardens and beautiful meadows, you will no doubt see groups of people walking together enjoying each other's company. Just past a sparkling fountain of rainbow colors you turn into the driveway of my home.

Inside, crystal bowls of fresh flowers are displayed in every room. (That was one of my dreams when I lived on earth.) Polished furniture and deep, soft chairs and couches make for comfortable living and relaxed entertaining. Everything is caressed by the cool Breath of Life as it comes through the open windows.

One of my favorite rooms is the library. It's filled with leather-bound treasures. Are you surprised that we have books in heaven? Haven't you found one of the joys of life is reading good books, and one of its frustrations is never having enough time to read everything you want to? I have two entire shelves of books by one of England's most beloved authors, Elizabeth

Goudge. I understand you were friends and you have a collection of her books in your home too. She arrived here several years ago. When I told her about my letters to you, she smiled and said she's looking forward to having you over to her lovely home for an old-fashioned English high tea. (Yes, you most certainly can have tea in heaven!)

All the rooms at the back of my home open onto a cool, shaded terrace. It's one of my favorite places. A vast expanse of soft, green lawn sweeps down to the creek bordering my garden. Flowers of every color reflect off each other, creating shades of iridescent beauty. Being limited to earthly words makes it impossible for me to describe the deep peace and contentment I find in the beautiful home God designed especially for me. I am continually filled with praise and never cease saying, "Thank you, Jesus."

What would your ideal heavenly home look like? Maybe you'd like a chalet perched among the alpine slopes. Or how about a lovely ocean cottage with a wide front porch. You could take long walks on the beach or swim with the dolphins. Or perhaps you'd like a gracious Southern mansion complete with tall white pillars and a wrap-around veranda where you could visit with loved ones and sip one of the heavenly drinks made from the fruits of the Tree of Life. Regardless of the type of home you prefer, please do not mistakenly picture heaven (like I used to) as one big crowded city where everyone lives in a lonely, cold mansion.

Heaven is a place of intricate design and infinite beauty. Filled with color and music that far exceed what you know now, it's a place of gardens and trees, fruits and grain. Of cities and countrysides, mountains and forests, beautiful homes and buildings. Of gates and streets, fountains and waterfalls. Heaven is a place of people and angels, love and laughter. And guess what? You don't even have to pack to come here!

It's also a place of worship. But I'll focus on that in another letter.

Yours from the Other Side

&

Dear Child of God,
Did you ever realize that the Bible starts out with paradise and ends with heaven?

That was a new thought to me and I wanted to share it with you before I got too far into this letter about the majesty of God and heaven. This insight made me realize how accurate God's Word is. Throughout the entire Bible there is a precise pattern of recorded historical events. Every story of every character is told with a methodical, marvelous progression. The Bible is a factual account of how God has worked through history and the way He continues to deal with the human race. From Genesis to Revelation, every page declares God's righteousness and love and points to His majesty. I enjoy writing these letters to you because they give me the opportunity to meditate on our great God and then to put thoughts on paper in a way you'll understand.

Today I want to give you just a brief peek into the wonder and majesty of God and His heaven. I'll share more in later letters, but let's get started with this interesting fact: *Heaven is a totally different form of existence from anything you've ever experienced.* It's in a totally different place. You might even say it's in a totally different dimension! It's difficult even to begin explaining the contrast between heaven and earth in your language. But it's somewhat like the difference between a little boy pretending he can make his model plane fly through the air and a giant Boeing 747 luxury jet soaring above him in the cloudless blue sky. Heaven is as different from earth as a small mud hut in the middle of a Brazilian jungle is different from a magnificent sprawling mansion on the white sands of Rio de Janeiro. Or contrast life for a small bird in the confines of a tiny, wire cage with the unlimited freedom and beauty this bird would experience if the cage door were suddenly thrown open in an enchanted forest.

Whatever comparison you prefer, the exciting truth is that heaven is where life is real at last—where all pure values such as love, justice, and peace are fully realized. It is the accumulation of all God planned for His creation before the foundation of the world. How large does a place have to be to contain the truth of God? That's hard to explain when you're still confined to earth, but Raymond Moody once said, "Heaven is big enough so that billions of races and billions of saved people are never crowded, yet small enough so that no one gets lost or lonely."[6] I like that, don't you?

Heaven is a place vibrant with fulfilling, creative activity, all done in obedience with God's plan. It's a place where you are always in God's presence and aware of His unceasing love and unequaled perfection, where Immanuel—God with us—is totally realized.

Every time I think of the greatness of God I'm reminded of that glorious night when He displayed His infinite majesty by visiting earth. It was a night when God, the Creator, became like the created; when God, the giver of life, left the glories of heaven to be born in a stable and placed in a feed trough in the little town of Bethlehem. What kind of love could possibly motivate such an act of wonder? It was God's everlasting, unconditional love for the human race. This expression of love is of such magnitude that even the angels bow their heads in awe. It's a love that no one on earth will ever fully understand, but all in heaven will continually experience. It's far beyond human comprehension.

When I try to describe heaven to you, I find it difficult to create word pictures of all I see and experience. One of your great theologians, Eugene Peterson, said it so well: "Heaven is a reality inaccessible at this point to any of our five senses."[7] It is like trying to describe a brilliant rainbow to a person blind from birth. You could see the iridescent colors, but you'd find it nearly impossible to put those same colors, transparent as the sunlight, into words that would mean anything to the blind person. And because heaven is a place where all is touched by the finger of God, it's better experienced than described.

All I can say is that heaven is beautiful beyond description. There is unspeakable joy and love beyond all measure. Heaven is filled with the majestic presence of God. It's so full of glory and majestic splendor that all we can do is fall on our knees in humble adoration and cry with a full heart, "My Lord and my God!"

All praise and honor and glory be unto Him forever and ever!

Yours from the Other Side

CHAPTER TWO

Where is Heaven?

Dear Child of God,

Have you ever wondered *where* heaven is? I used to think about this question when I lived on earth. I'd look up into a moonlit sky strung with diamonds and wonder, *Is heaven up there?* Sometimes when the swirling colors of a dazzling sunset touched the earth with warmth and beauty, I was sure that the curtain of heaven had parted just a little and some of its glory had slipped out. Other times when looking at the sunlit clouds brushed with gold, I could almost hear the angels blowing trumpets, and for a fleeting moment, I actually expected to see Jesus coming among trailing clouds of glory. I'm sure you've had similar experiences from time to time.

But *where is heaven?* That's a difficult question to answer from here, but I'll try. First of all, heaven is located in a totally different world. In my earlier letters I've described some of the physical aspects of heaven and affirmed that heaven has a precise location.

But no one from earth has ever found heaven. Not when the spaceship *Pioneer 1* went 70,000 miles into orbit. Not when the Russians went 373,000 miles into outer space. Not one of the astronauts found heaven when *Pioneer 4* journeyed through 400,000 miles of space. No one sent back a message announcing, "We've found it! We just saw the pearly gates! Another giant step for humankind!"

With the Hubble Space Telescope, one of the scientific wonders at the end of the twentieth century, scientists have observed and recorded the death of stars billions of light years away from the earth. In spite of the ability to peer into space as never before, no one on earth has found the biblical heaven.

So *where is heaven?* Is it light years away from the earth? Could it be above the atmosphere and beyond interplanetary space? Is it beyond the millions of galaxies in your universe or above the trillions of stars? Unfortunately even if I answered these questions, my answers would not really be to your satisfaction because heaven is in another dimension. But one thing I can tell you for sure, heaven is as close to you as your next breath!

You might say heaven is in a fifth dimension separated from your world by nothing but a thin veil. You know from Scripture and true-life angel stories you've read or experienced that heaven can't be too far away because angels are continually coming and going between heaven and earth. They know each time someone is born into the family of God and rejoice over every sinner who repents.[1] They instantly record the name of each new believer in the Book of Life.[2] The Bible tells you that you're under God's care and His angels are assigned to guard you in all your ways.[3] They often come to rescue you in a split second.

Jacob, one of the Old Testament patriarchs, once referred to a ladder or stairway into heaven where he saw angels going up and down between earth and heaven. This is an example of how close heaven is. When speaking of heaven Jesus said, "There are no more barriers between heaven and earth, earth and heaven."[4] This thin veil that separates you from heaven is a wonderful, yet perplexing truth to understand. Right now you still live in a body made of flesh and blood. There's no way you can walk through a wall as Jesus did after His resurrection. Nor can you walk through the veil that separates heaven from earth.

But never forget the promise Jesus gave to the thief on the cross: "Today you will be with me in paradise." Now that's fast! When Paul was caught up into heaven, he went there and back in one day. The Bible states that when Jesus comes again, those believers remaining on earth will be changed in a moment, in the twinkling of an eye.[5] These concepts are incomprehensible to you right now because you're still held captive by space, time, and gravity. However, be assured of this truth: Heaven is very near. It's as real as the city you live in today. And it's a place teeming with life. Theologian and author Edward Bounds called it a "city of life."[6] And oh, what a life!

Where is heaven? The Bible refers to it by using the specific direction of *up*.[7] That's because God knew you could identify with that idea. He also says that someday Jesus will come *down* from heaven with a shout and the sound of a trumpet. All believers on earth at that time will be caught up to meet the Lord in the air and remain with Him forever.[8] What a great promise!

Where is heaven? It's where God lives. It's His kingdom. It's a place of total joy and lasting life. Heaven is where Jesus is. It's also where all believers will be someday. Jesus said, "I will . . . take you to be with me, that you also may be where I am."[9] What an honor God has given you and all who believe in Him. When Jesus ascended into heaven, a cloud covered Him from the disciples' view. They didn't see an elevator or spaceship. He simply raised His hands up toward heaven and before their astonished eyes, He began to glide slowly up.[10] After He was gone, angels appeared (maybe standing on the invisible heavenly stairway) and asked a question that seemed perfectly natural to them: "Why do you just stand here looking up at an empty sky? This very Jesus who was taken up from among you to heaven will come as certainly—and mysteriously—as he left."[11]

Where is heaven? It's a place of joy where you will be with Jesus, the Light of the world and the Light of all glory.[12] Your joy of being with Him will always be preeminent. The very center of heaven is a Person—the King of kings and Lord of lords—your great Creator, Savior, Redeemer. Heaven is where you see Jesus face to face. It is where the accumulation of all the promises of God are fully known and understood.

Heaven is where God reigns.

Yours from the Other Side

❧

Dear Child of God,

My last letter ended on such a high note of glory with Jesus as King of kings and Lord of lords — with heaven being the place where God reigns — that I suddenly realized how easy it is to forget you still live in a world filled with sin and sorrow, misery and death. I found myself forgetting about God's greatest enemy, the Devil, who continues to race throughout the whole earth like a roaring lion, seeking those he can deceive and destroy.[13] I forget about the insatiable hatred he has for you and all of God's beloved children. I forget, sitting securely up here, that you are faced with daily battles against the evil forces of your world.

Please forgive me. And please know that I pray daily for a shield of God's protection to surround you and keep you from the evil one. Jesus prayed that same request for His disciples and all those who would follow Him when He prayed in the garden just before His crucifixion.[14]

Heaven is a place where you won't experience the difficult things of earth. First and most important of all, you'll never again experience the power of the Devil because he isn't in heaven. And because there's no devil here, there isn't any sin or evil. Heaven is absolutely free from every consequence of sin.

Furthermore, there's no perversion or pornography and all the evil and sorrow that go with them. No more drunkenness, drugs, or drug dealers sapping the life from God's most precious creation — people. There are no wars — no land stained with innocent blood. No murder, rape, torture, incest, or blasphemy. No violence of any kind. Because there's no sin to spoil the beauty and wonder of God's creation, all is total perfection. I can almost hear you shouting "Hallelujah" from way up here!

Heaven is also a place where there are no worries, no house payments, no car payments, no taxes, and no credit cards. In fact, there are no debts at all! There's no gossip, no lying, no cheating. You'll never see the face of an abused or starving child, or homeless people wandering cold, dark, lonely streets. It's a place where every wrong is made right.

And as good as all this is, there's something even more wonderful. You'll never see a hospital or cemetery because there's no pain, no sickness, no disease, and no death. No people with blind eyes and deaf ears. No more old, wrinkled, aching bodies. You'll no longer live in a place saturated with suffering and the fear that comes with it. There are no funerals or separation. No loneliness or broken hearts. You'll never again be parted from your loved ones who have trusted in Christ for redemption.

And there are no more tears. With tenderness God will wipe them all from your eyes. There's no disappointment in heaven.

From what I've told you, you know that heaven is not simply a transformed earth with all of its earthiness suddenly glorified. Nor is it some kind of perfected Garden of Eden. Just as it's impossible to explain to an unborn child what life will be outside the womb, it's impossible to fully describe heaven to you before you get here.

But I can tell you this. Here is joy without sorrow, rest without weariness, and life ever new. All this and so much more is what your loving heavenly Father has waiting for you. It's enough to make you fall on your knees before Him in worship and adoration, crying with a full heart, "Holy, holy, holy." Someday you'll do just that!

Yours from the Other Side

CHAPTER THREE
What's the Way to Heaven?

Dear Child of God,

It's great that you've joined a small-group Bible study. I wish everyone on earth could be part of one. You will come to mean so much to each other as you study and pray together. This group will be especially helpful to you in light of your father's progressing illness. You'll receive encouragement in the months ahead as they walk through this difficult time with you.

Your group has a good variety of people with different interests and backgrounds. It's good that some have been following Christ for a long time, others are new to this way of living, and some are honestly searching for answers to major questions of life. That's what I call a healthy mix!

Thank you for asking me to be a part of the group through my letters. Thanks too for sharing the questions they want to study in the next few weeks. The questions go right to the heart of the Christian faith, and the answers are the foundation for all future study. You said you all agreed that there is a God. But then there was quite a bit of discussion about what He's like. Some wondered how to teach their children about God.

This letter and my next one will help answer your key questions: *What is God like?* and *How can we be sure we'll be with Him in heaven?*

We can learn much about God by looking at His creation. Have you found it strange that scientists know how to measure the stars, land on the moon, and foretell when the next eclipse is due right down to the very day and even the precise minute? All of these things are possible because scientists understand that the universe operates on precise, fixed laws. It's an accepted fact that everything in the universe takes place within the boundaries of those rules. Scientists know that when these laws are broken, there's a price to be paid.

Just as science and the physical universe have fixed laws, God operates on precise, absolute, moral laws. When His laws are broken, there's also a price to be paid. God's laws are called the Ten Commandments.[1] (Your group might like to memorize them.) These are exact rules—not suggestions—of how life should be lived in your relationship with God and one another. That's why the Bible says they're to be written on your heart.[2] Jesus summed up all ten of the commandments by saying we should love God and one another. Now that sounds fairly easy to do. But the truth is that people on earth break God's moral laws every day. The obvious result is that they live in a world of broken relationships between each other and between themselves and God.

What is God like? The answer to that question is revealed in one of the most profound statements you'll ever read about God. It sums up exactly what He's like: "God so loved the world that he gave his one and only Son, that whoever believes in him shall not perish but have eternal life."[3] Everything you ever need to know about God is wrapped up in that one amazing truth. From it you learn two important truths: God is a *loving* God and God is a *giving* God.

In no other religion in the history of the world has there ever been a god who loved in this way. The depth of God's love is beyond human comprehension.

The problem is that the world God loves so much is totally opposite from all that He is. He calls this problem *sin*. Now I agree, sin is a word you don't hear mentioned very often on earth anymore. No one wants to talk about it, few ministers speak about it, and people no longer seem to believe it exists. Seldom is it taken seriously, and it has almost slipped unnoticed from the vocabulary.

What is sin? Does anyone really believe in sin anymore? Is anyone guilty of it? Is sin simply making a mistake? Or is it only when you do something really wrong or commit some horrible crime? Is it just unacceptable behavior? Your group asked some good questions. The problem is not what you *do*, the problem is who you *are*. Who you are—a sinner— makes you do what you do—sin. God tells us, "All have sinned and fall short of the glory of God."[4]

To help see how widespread this problem of sin is, just think for a moment of what you read in yesterday's newspaper or saw on the news. Then recall what was in last week's paper, last month's, last year's, and all the ones before that. Then think about what you'll read or hear tomorrow, next week, next month, next year. Believe me, you'll find evidence of sin! Every day the news spews forth torrid accounts of killing, rape, sorrow, heartache, and slaughter. These are followed by accounts of drug and alcohol abuse, incest, beatings, and untold ways people have concocted to torture one another. One of the men in your group told of a young man who knowingly exposed dozens of young girls to the AIDS virus. That same paper reported that a thirteen-year-old boy murdered his mother "just to see what it was like to kill someone." The welfare worker in your group told how she is trying to find a home for eight children who were abandoned in a run-down, filthy apartment. It seems the world is rapidly sinking into a cesspool of greed, hate, jealousy, and perversion. God calls all of this *sin*.

Your group concluded that the list of man's inhumanity is an insatiable record of horror. One of the reasons behind all this is that there's no longer any fear of God and, as a result, fear of one another grows ever more pervasive. One of your group members mentioned that in many instances of recorded history, Nietzsche's description of the human race as "vermin on the crust of the earth" can be understood. When you think of the Holocaust and of the ethnic cleansing at the end of the twentieth century, and when you consider that out of the thousands of years of recorded history only thirty-five have been without war and bloodshed, it becomes easier to accept God's indictment against humanity: "All have sinned." A good way to sum up sin is this: Sin separates you from God. It is the opposite of all that God is.

Whew! Stick with me. I know these letters are supposed to be about heaven, but we can't talk about heaven without first considering the problem of sin. No one can get to heaven (the topic of my next letter) until sin has been taken care of. But you can't take care of it by yourself. The good news is that God knows that, and two thousand years ago He sent

Jesus to pay the price of breaking God's moral laws for you. He left heaven and came to earth for one reason only—to die on the cross as payment for your sin and mine, and all those who believe. When Jesus was on earth, He walked the streets, ate food, talked human languages, and showed humankind the meaning and purpose of life. He taught the significance of truth, goodness, and love. He showed us how to live and how to die. When He finished teaching all our finite minds could understand, He went to the cross where He died to pay the penalty for our sin. Jesus rose again on the third day, conquering for all time and eternity two of the greatest enemies on earth—sin and death.

He came to restore the fellowship that was lost because of sin. He came to give clear, concise directions on how you can know Him as your Savior and Lord. He came to show you the way to heaven—this beautiful place He prepared for you. God took the initiative, but you have a part too. I look forward to sharing in my next letter how you can be sure you're on the right road.

Yours from the Other Side

✖

Dear Child of God,

It's good to hear how well your group is going. I smiled when you said you set aside an hour for study and two hours later you were all still talking and no one wanted to go home.

You said you were "riveted to your Bibles and questions were flying back and forth." I could almost hear the wheels turning in everyone's minds! I can assure you, you're becoming possessors of life-changing knowledge.

You remember in my last letter I mentioned what God has done to take care of the problem of sin. Now here's more of the good news: This letter will be about what you must do to take care of your sin.

In your lifetime you'll receive many wonderful gifts from family and friends. But by far the greatest gift you'll ever receive is God's gift of unconditional love and forgiveness. It's a gift of such vast proportion that it exceeds the intellectual capacities of the most brilliant minds. Yet it's a gift of such simplicity that even a child can understand and receive it. You don't have to pay for it — there's no price tag attached. You can't earn it by self-sacrifice or by following a set of rules — no amount of good works is enough or too little. You can be sick and dying and so weak you can hardly breathe, or you can be as strong as an Olympian athlete. You can be a billionaire or a pauper. God's gift is freely given and must be freely received.

Today the world seems indifferent to this gracious gift of God. But God knew this would happen when He took the risk of creating people with the freedom of choice — when He created us as thinking, rational, moral beings. He could have created us like puppets on strings, but instead He chose to give each person the freedom of choice. What each of us chooses to believe about Jesus matters eternally. How tragic to think it's only a personal choice that either keeps us from heaven or guarantees our reservation. Peter Kreeft said, "It is the seeking heart that determines our eternal destiny."5 And God tells us that all who seek Him will find Him. What a promise!

I'm so glad you asked me to share God's message of love and forgiveness in a simple way. I learned long ago (when I lived on earth) that happiness is knowing God and understanding what you believe. With that knowledge comes a deep sense of contentment and peace. But what should you believe? And what should you share with others about Jesus?

As I wrote last time, the first step is agreeing with God that you are a sinner and that only He can take away your sin through Jesus' death on the cross. Have you noticed that wherever you go in the world today, a cross is often displayed on churches? It serves as a continual reminder to every passerby that Jesus provided the only remedy for sin. It is only the blood of Jesus Christ that cleanses you from sin. God freely offers forgiveness to all who receive His gift of Jesus as Savior and Lord.

That's the gospel—or good news—in a nutshell. As you study with your group each week, these truths will sink deep within your hearts, and you'll have the joy of sharing them with others outside your group. The more you understand these basic truths, the less fear you'll have about sharing them.

You asked me to give you a simple definition of what it means to follow Christ. You wanted one that the group members could share with their children and grandchildren. How wonderful! So many people expect the Sunday school teacher or youth director to do this. It's so important that children hear the beautiful truth of God's love from their parents.

What is a Christian? A Christian is one in whom God dwells. That's it! It's so basic and yet so profound that it staggers the mind to consider it. God has made it so simple. We're the ones who've made it complicated. Of course, there are many wonderful truths that make up the Christian life. Here are four of them.

1. *A Christian is one who chooses, by an act of will, to receive Jesus Christ as Savior and Lord.* Long before anyone chooses to follow Jesus, God works through the Holy Spirit to help that person want to choose Him and have a relationship with Him. Remember this: Christianity isn't a religion—it's a relationship. And the relationship is with the living God.

2. *You know that God is working in your life when you realize you're on the wrong road of life and you want to get on the right road with Jesus.* In Bible terms it means you *repent*. Some people don't like or understand that word because they think it sounds old-fashioned or negative. But repentance is always positive and brings positive results. It simply means you acknowledge that you have chosen to do things your own way and that you want to turn around and do things God's way.

3. *To receive God's gift of salvation means to be forgiven*—one of the most beautiful words in any language. To be forgiven means to have your wrong attitudes and actions (or sin) taken away as though they never happened. It means the record of your life is swept clean, like when you sweep the

floor or hit the delete button on a computer. It means living in the joy of being completely forgiven every day. This is made possible only through the death of Jesus on the cross to pay the penalty for your sin and the sin of the world. God's amazing promise to you is this: "The blood of Jesus, his Son, purifies us from all sin."[6]

4. *When you receive God's gift, you become a member of God's family.* The way this happens is beautiful in its simplicity. Jesus said, "Here I am, I stand at the door and knock. If anyone hears my voice and opens the door, I will come in."[7] That door is the door of your life. The moment you open that door and ask Jesus to come in, you are born into the family of God. Your name is written in the Book of Life in heaven and the angels praise God because of you![8] That's good news! Believe me, it's the best news you or anyone else will ever hear.

Here's a delightful story that illustrates this truth. It may help your group members when they are telling their children about God's love. Once long ago, there was a little boy who spent the long winter months building a boat to sail on the lake in a nearby park. The boy painted his boat a shiny, candy-apple red and trimmed it with white sails. It was a work of art in his eyes. At last the boat was finished and spring arrived. His mother packed him a lunch and sent him off to the park. When the boy reached the lake, joy filled every part of his body. Today he would launch his boat!

As he stooped to set it on the water, he made sure the string was tied securely so he wouldn't lose it. How pretty the sailboat looked as it bounced up and down on the water.

But it wasn't long before a great gust of wind tore the string from the boy's hand. In horror, he watched his little boat sail out to the middle of the lake, around the bend, and out of sight. All day long the little boy ran up and down the shore searching for his boat. At nightfall he turned home broken-hearted.

Throughout the summer, he continued to search for his boat, but it was gone. One autumn day the little boy went to the village square. In one of the shop windows he saw his lost sailboat. He burst through the door and asked the shop owner to return it to him. But the old man told him he had bought it just the day before. He said the boy could have it if he paid five dollars—an enormous sum for any small boy. So the boy ran all the way home, emptied his bank, and searched his pockets until he found all the money he had. It was the exact amount he needed. He ran back to the store as fast as he could and gave the owner the money. The boat belonged to him again. As he left the shop, he hugged his little sailboat and through happy tears whispered, "Don't you see? You are twice mine! I made you, you were lost, and I bought you back!"

That's exactly what God did for you. He made you. Then you rebelled against Him—went your own way—and ignored Him. You were lost in sin. Jesus came to earth to seek and to save all who are lost. When He found you, He bought you back by giving all He had—His very life.

John Bunyan, that great author of *Pilgrim's Progress*, said it so well:

To see a prince entreat a beggar to receive an alms, would be a strange sight; to see a king entreat the traitor to accept mercy, would be a stranger sight than that, but to see God entreat a sinner, to hear Christ say, "I stand at the door and knock," with a heart full and a heaven full of grace to bestow upon all who opens: this is such a sight as dazzles the eyes of angels. . . .[9]

Are you dazzled by God's glorious plan of salvation? Are you dazzled by the truth that heaven's gate is open to all who accept the gift of God through Jesus Christ the Lord? Are you dazzled by the fact that when you actively receive this gift, your name is written in the Book of Life and can never be erased? Are you dazzled with the knowledge that you then become a citizen of heaven?

Do you know that when you receive Jesus as Savior and Lord, He gives you:

- ◆ new birth
- ◆ new heart
- ◆ new name
- ◆ new desire
- ◆ new life
- ◆ new home
- ◆ new purpose for living

What you choose to do with God's plan and His gift of salvation matters eternally. His words are true.

How can you be sure you're on your way to heaven?

Simply by agreeing with God that you've gone your own way, asking for forgiveness, accepting Christ's death on the cross as payment for your sin debt, and thanking Him for His answer. Then you can be assured you won't miss heaven.

Here's a simple prayer much like the one everyone in heaven has prayed:

> Lord Jesus, thank You for dying on the cross to pay the penalty for my sin. Please forgive all my sins and make me clean and whole within. Come into my life and be my Savior and Lord. I receive Your gift of salvation and eternal life. Fill me with Your Holy Spirit and make me all You created me to be. Thank You for loving me and coming to live within me. In Your name, Amen.

Yours from the Other Side

&

Dear Child of God,

I trust after reading my last letter you'll never have to say, "I *hope* I am going to heaven." God wants you to *know* for certain that you are. He wants you to have an inner peace that comes with His absolute assurance that once you accept the gift of salvation and forgiveness, you belong to the family of God. His love for you is complete and eternal. He said, "I have loved you with an everlasting love."[10] That's God's promise to you.

To help you understand just how certain He wants you to be about His forgiveness and the place He has reserved for you in heaven, here's a list to remind you of His promises:[11]

- ◆ He has given you His plan, and you have received it.
- ◆ He has given you His gift of salvation, and you have gratefully accepted it.
- ◆ You have committed your life into His loving care.
- ◆ You are a new creation in Christ.
- ◆ You have been born into the family of God.
- ◆ You are His beloved child.
- ◆ You have been forgiven and the relationship with God that was broken by sin is now restored.
- ◆ Your name is written in the Book of Life with the blood of Jesus and can never be erased.
- ◆ You have a promised inheritance that will never perish, rust, or spoil, nor be stolen or lost.
- ◆ You are an heir of God and a "joint-heir with Christ."
- ◆ Your acceptance of the finished work of Christ on the cross is your guarantee to heaven.
- ◆ Your relationship and fellowship with the living God is a never-ending source of joy.
- ◆ This is the glorious truth of God's Word to you, anchored to the Rock—Jesus Christ—for all time and eternity.

These promises from God are yours to carry with you as you journey through life. Go over them often until they become a part of your life. Write them down and give them to your children or friends. Claim them with joy.

The real joy of heaven isn't in all the things you receive or are going to receive. As wonderful as they are, the eternal joy of heaven is what you'll be like when you get here. God has promised us, "We shall be like him, for we shall see him as he is."[12]

All the beauties and wonders of heaven are secondary. The ultimate joy is being with Jesus. I'll be writing more about this in my next few letters.

Yours from the Other Side

CHAPTER FOUR
What Will We Be Like?

Dear Child of God,

Thanks for your response to my last letter. You raised some good questions that many people ask. Your first question was an excellent one: *What will I do in heaven?* Before I answer this one, I need to answer your other question: *What will I be like in heaven?* It will take me several letters to cover each of these great questions. Remember, I'm limited to the vocabulary of earth. Believe me, this letter could be more difficult to write than I originally anticipated!

Let's see. *What will you be like in heaven?* Perhaps an example might help. Do you remember when you were little how you would watch with amazement as a caterpillar slowly spun a cocoon around itself on a tree in your back yard? That dried-up chrysalis would hang on the branch for several days or weeks. Then one day the ugly caterpillar would break through the shell and a glorious butterfly would emerge and soar away into the sky. When that happened, a metamorphosis occurred. The caterpillar-worm had been transformed into the graceful beauty of a butterfly—"a flower with wings" or a "flying jewel" as poets have described them.

This is just a tiny glimpse into what happens after death. The natural body is placed in a cocoon-like coffin, but the real person—the real you—will emerge in the flawless beauty of the heavenly body God designed for you. It will be healed; it will be whole; it will be perfect; it will be new; it will be wonderful. You'll dance with joy when you receive it!

What was once a natural body is now a spiritual one. But you remain a real person in a real body, not some wispy puff of vapor floating around for eternity. Can you imagine a body free from all sin and disease, a new incorruptible body fit to live in a new heavenly place? Think what that means! On earth your physical body begins to die the moment you are born. You wage a daily struggle to care for it. You must feed it, give it water, keep it warm enough or cool enough, keep it from being broken or crushed, and guard it against disease. The contrast between your earthly body and your heavenly body is like the difference between ugliness and beauty, hate and love, night and day, incompleteness and wholeness, or a shadow and the actual object. Your earthly body is perishable. Your heavenly body will be imperishable.[1]

Think back to your ninth-grade biology class when you learned some interesting facts about your physical body. You were taught that every seven years you got an almost complete makeover. All the cells in your circulatory system and your flesh are different ones than you had a few years ago. This means the substance of your body changes about ten times during your lifetime, even though you have one hundred trillion cells all working together each day in perfect harmony. In spite of these remarkable changes, you're not a different person. The real you—your essence—remains the same. You retain the same personality, keep the same memories, and preserve the same identity. This is a grand mystery.

As the Psalmist said, you are indeed "fearfully and wonderfully made."[2]

The Message, one of your contemporary paraphrases of God's Word, describes this truth like this:

> You plant a 'dead' seed; soon there is a flourishing plant. There is no visual likeness between seed and plant. You could never guess what a tomato would look like by looking at a tomato seed. What we plant in the soil and what grows out of it don't look anything alike. The dead body that we bury in the ground and the resurrection body that comes from it will be dramatically different.[3]

As a gardener you witness this phenomenon every year when you plant your garden. All those little brown seeds you bury in the dirt soon become jewel-colored flowers or delicious vegetables. You can't fully explain it and neither can anyone else. How does a tall, majestic oak tree come from a tiny brown acorn in the ground? Because God designed it that way.

Does this help you understand a little better what happens to you when you die? Your physical body dies, and in a moment you receive a glorious new resurrected body in heaven. You are changed from the natural to the supernatural, from the corruptible to the incorruptible. God revealed this truth in the Bible.

Earthly bodies grow old, get tired, become wrinkled, and lose hair. They get weary, hungry, thirsty, and sick. They may need glasses or false teeth. They need vitamins and often numerous other pills throughout a lifetime. When they die, they return to dust. Some bodies die a natural death and are buried. Others drown in the sea and decay or are eaten by sea life. Still others are blown apart by bombs or crushed in auto accidents. It doesn't matter if your earthly body is destroyed at death because God has a new one planned for you. As a believer the real *you* receives this new body for all eternity.

What's this new body like? As I've said, it is imperishable. It is also pure and full of glory and power.[4] It's full of truth and dignity. In this new body, you'll have boundless energy to run and walk, laugh and sing, work and play. You'll use all of your intellectual and creative abilities to their fullest. You'll have an inexhaustible capacity for joy. You'll be totally content, fulfilled, and satisfied. Your body and soul will be perfectly united. Your new body will be perfectly adapted to the glory of heaven. It's far greater than you can ever imagine!

You'll have an infinite capacity for variety and creativity. And you will be filled with songs of praise and be all God created you to be.

This is the wonder of heaven!

Yours from the Other Side

❦

Dear Child of God,
I was happy to hear my last letter was helpful, especially the illustration of the butterfly and the interesting facts about the wonderful way God created you. You said it gave you the

beginning of an entirely new picture of what you'll be like in heaven. That's my desire in writing to you—to clear up some of the questions many people on earth have about heaven.

Today I'll tackle your question, *What will I be like in heaven?* The best way to do that is to remember what God has already revealed. Looking at what Jesus was like after His resurrection can give you some idea of what you'll be like.

Think in general about the incidents when Christ appeared following His death. From those recorded events we learn some specific things about what He was like. Remember how Jesus returned from the tomb in a completely new body? Still He was the same wonderful Jesus the disciples had lived with and studied under for three years. He looked the same. His personality and mannerisms hadn't changed. Yet He wasn't the same. He had a body like no one had ever seen on earth. He could suddenly appear and disappear as He did on the road to Emmaus. He could walk through walls and locked doors with nonchalant ease. He could glide through the air to heaven. At the same time, He had a body His disciples could touch.[5] He could talk to them and walk with them down the dusty Galilean roads. He enjoyed being with them in times of close fellowship and sharing. These are just a few examples of what Christ's body was like during the forty days He was on earth after His resurrection.

As I wrote last time, you too will have a wonderful new body! These true stories about Jesus' new body give you some idea of what your new body will be like. It will have a heavenly substance and yet be tangible. With your new body you'll be able to talk with God and other people in heaven and to walk the golden paths of heaven with your loved ones. You'll enjoy times of fellowship with friends and family and, best of all, with Jesus. Although your spiritual body will be able to do many things you can't do now, you'll still be recognizable as *you*.

I can almost hear your next questions, *But will I look the same? And what about the ninety-five percent of people who don't like the way they look now?* I remember struggling with that on earth. It seems like everyone wants to look different than they do. They want to be more beautiful or more handsome. Some wish they weren't so fat or so skinny. Those with blue eyes want brown ones, those with curly hair want straight hair, and on it goes. Believe me, I understand because I used to have some of the same thoughts. Let me assure you, those thoughts don't continue once you get here.

There's another side of what you'll be like in heaven. It has to do with your words and actions. In heaven your actions and words will be purified but expressed through the same personality you have on earth. Consider two accounts about Jesus after His resurrection that demonstrate this truth.

The first one deals with Thomas, the one disciple who was honest enough to put his doubts into words.[6] He said he couldn't believe Jesus had risen from the grave unless he could see Him and touch the nail prints. And so Jesus made a special appearance to Thomas. He showed Thomas the scars in His hands and the wound in His side where the soldier had thrust the spear. Then in a voice full of love for His doubting disciple, Jesus commanded him to reach out and touch the nail prints with his own hands. (There weren't any heavy sighs of impatience or rolled eyes with Jesus.) And it was in that moment of dynamic reality that all of Thomas's doubts vanished forever. He did the only thing he could do: He fell on his knees and cried out in desperate humility, "My Lord and my God!" And his life was never the same. His doubts were gone because he knew the One who appeared to him was the same One who had died.

And how did Thomas know he was talking with Jesus? He was certain because Jesus dealt with him in the same way He would have *before* the Resurrection. Christ demonstrated the same tender compassion and thoughtfulness because these traits are part of His character. His personality and essence are always the same.[7] Throughout His life and after His resurrection Jesus always modeled perfect love, joy, peace, patience, kindness, goodness, faithfulness, gentleness, and self-control.[8] All believers have this same fruit of the Spirit. On earth they often use these gifts imperfectly, but in heaven they will use them perfectly. Can you imagine what you'll be like when all love, joy, peace, and patience come to fruition in you? Because you will still have your own personality, the way these traits will be revealed through you in heaven will be unique to you. All of these qualities will be wrapped up and expressed in the beauty of your new body, and you'll become all that God created you to be.

Now think of the time when Jesus appeared to seven of the disciples after they'd been fishing all night without success. Remember how discouraged they were? It seemed all their dreams lay shattered. The One they had followed so closely was gone. They felt life would never be the same again. So they returned to the only thing they knew to do—fishing.

What a sorry group! Even after fishing all night, their nets were empty. It was then that Jesus appeared to them in the light of early dawn. There He stood on the beach with a heart full of compassion. The disciples were out in the deep water hoping for even one fish in their nets. Jesus called out to them to cast their nets on the other side of the boat. What a strange request! But the disciples did so and instantly the net was filled with 153 fish.[9]

Jesus knew the men were hungry so He fixed them a delicious breakfast right there on the beach. He then ate with them and talked with them. No one had to ask who He was because they recognized Him by the way He looked and how He related to them.

I hope both of these examples give you an idea of what you'll be like in heaven. You'll relate to God and to your fellow heavenly citizens in such a way that they'll all know that you are *you*.

Now let's go back to an event that took place during Jesus' earthly life that reveals Him in all His heavenly glory and helps you understand another aspect of what you'll be like in heaven. It's the beautiful story of Jesus on the Mount of Transfiguration. Jesus had taken Peter, James, and John up the mountain where He continued to teach them without the many crowds that constantly followed Him.[10] While there, "His appearance changed from the inside out, right before their eyes. Sunlight poured from his face. His clothes were filled with light. Then they realized that Moses and Elijah were also there in deep conversation with him . . . a light-radiant cloud enveloped them, and sounding from deep in the cloud a voice: 'This is my Son, marked by my love, focus of my delight. Listen to him.' When the disciples heard it, they fell flat on their faces, scared to death. But Jesus came over and touched them. 'Don't be afraid.' When they opened their eyes and looked around all they saw was Jesus, only Jesus."

Imagine what that was like. One moment the disciples were simply listening to Jesus and the next they saw heaven's radiance as the thin veil was pulled aside. They saw our Lord revealed in all His righteousness with His body and clothing arrayed in dazzling white splendor, and they saw Moses and Elijah "in glorious splendor."[11] The entire scene was covered in God's glory. The three disciples had a glimpse of what they (and you!) would be like in heaven. When talking about the end of the age, Jesus said, "Then the righteous will shine like the sun in the kingdom of their Father."[12] The prophet Daniel had a hint of this when the Lord told him, "Those who are wise will shine like the brightness of the heavens, and those who lead many to righteousness, like the stars for ever and ever."[13]

In heaven you too will be dressed in the glorious robes of the righteousness of Jesus Christ.[14] You will wear these robes not because you are deity, but because God has chosen to clothe you in them since you placed your trust in His Son. As C. S. Lewis said, you will be "strong, radiant, wise, beautiful and drenched in joy."[15] Yes, the glory of God's presence will cover you and all of heaven throughout eternity.

This, dear child of God, is what you will be like.

Yours from the Other Side

✍

Dear Child of God,

It's good to know my last two letters helped clarify what you will be like in heaven. From your earthly perspective it's hard to imagine how you can be so changed and yet be the same you. Most people wonder about that. Your next question, *Will I recognize my loved ones?*, is a natural follow-up to your previous one. And it's definitely easier to answer!

Reunions with loved ones and friends you haven't seen for a long time are always met with great enthusiasm. Remember seeing your childhood friend after being separated for many years? You embraced and both shouted at once, "You haven't changed a bit! I'd have known you anywhere!" No introductions were needed even though you both looked quite different. You picked up as though you'd been together only the day before. You had instant rapport, instant joy, instant excitement, instant memories, and instant fellowship. You knew each other immediately. That's the way it is in heaven all the time.

The answer to your question, *Will I recognize my loved ones in heaven?*, is a loud resounding *yes!* Scottish author George MacDonald responded to that question with a touch of dry humor, "Shall we be greater fools in Paradise than we are here?"

You'll know them in the same way Peter, James, and John recognized Moses and Elijah on the mountain top even though they'd never met. No one questioned who they were. The disciples simply knew. Moses and Elijah were easily recognizable. And Moses and Elijah knew each other even though they didn't live on earth at the same time. In fact,

Moses lived almost seven hundred years before Elijah, yet there they were talking together like old friends.

Not only will you have the inexpressible joy of seeing and recognizing your loved ones, but you'll also recognize those people who ministered to you while you lived on earth. You'll see the Sunday school teacher who faithfully taught you the Bible accounts of David and Goliath, Joseph and his coat of many colors, and Daniel in the lions' den.

You'll see the blind evangelist, Dr. Walter Kallenbach, who preached a message on John 3 one summer evening so long ago. You were only ten years old, but you knew you wanted to give your life to Jesus. And even though you were shy, you got up from your seat and walked alone down that long church aisle to receive Jesus as Savior and Lord. Dr. Kallenbach is here in heaven now, and he's no longer blind. I saw him recently. He told me he remembered the child who took his hand and said in a voice choked with tears, "I want to know Jesus." He's delighted to hear you've been walking with Jesus all these years and is looking forward to seeing you in God's time.

You'll see and recognize all the people who helped you grow in your walk with the Lord on earth. Think for a minute how many expressed God's love to you in countless ways— all who loved you and prayed for you. There are many you're probably not even aware of who prayed faithfully for you through the years. What joy you will feel when you're reunited. You'll have the opportunity to thank them for guiding you along the way.

As wonderful as those experiences will be, there's an even

greater joy waiting for you when you see and recognize the people with whom you had the privilege of sharing the gospel. Remember your school friends and the long discussions you had about God? Several of those friends became Christians and their names are written in the Book of Life.

Think about the variety of people in your small group. Imagine the many ways they have unknowingly given God's love to others.

Think of the young second-grade teacher who always says a quick prayer for each child as he or she enters the classroom. She never feels she's doing much, but from God's perspective, she's giving those children an important gift — the gift of prayer. When she arrives in heaven many years from now, she'll be surprised at the miraculous ways God will have used her prayers to reach those children with His love.

Then there's the Sunday school teacher who has taught sixth-grade boys for almost ten years. (That can be a challenge in itself!) When he arrives in heaven, he'll never tire of listening to the stories of how God changed the lives of those boys entrusted to his care.

Another special person in your group is the single mother who works at the hospital as a nurse. I wish you could see the tender, gentle way she cares for her patients. They say the room lights up when she walks in. Because she deals with life and death matters much of the time, patients often ask if she'll pray with them. Believe me, she has a whole host of people waiting to thank her when she arrives here someday.

One of the couples who meets with you each week have opened their home to pregnant teenagers who don't have any place else to go. Many of these girls have turned their lives around as they respond to the love and wise counsel they receive. And many babies have been given the gift of life because their young mothers had support and a place to live. Think of all the thank-yous waiting for this couple in heaven someday!

I have a word of encouragement for you too. Remember when you lived in Brazil? Once a week you'd go to the *favelas* where the poorest of the poor lived. The children would come from all the surrounding cardboard "houses" to hear Bible stories and learn happy songs. Many of these children were born into the family of God as a result. Some are here now; the rest will come later. I saw little Luiz Celso the other day. He drowned shortly after you left Brazil. I wish you could see him now. Instead of a tummy swollen from hunger and worms, he's filled with the joy of the Lord. His eyes sparkle with life and he has a smile you wouldn't believe!

These are just some of the "cups of cold water" your small group has given in the name of Jesus that are never forgotten.[16] There really is a story behind each person in your group. They've shown God's love in so many ways that they may not even be aware of. Maybe as your group gets to know one another better, you can share some of the stories. That will be a great encouragement to each of you.

Back to your question. Yes, you will recognize your loved ones in heaven. There will be great times of happy reunions and many shouts of joy. But the reunions that will bring the greatest joy are with people you told about the love of Jesus. They will welcome you home with songs of thanksgiving much like this one:

I dreamed I went to heaven, you were there with me,
We walked upon the streets of gold beside the crystal sea.
We heard the angels singing, then someone called your name;
You turned and saw this young man, he was smiling as he came.
And he said, "Friend, you may not know me now."
Then he said, "But wait!
You used to teach my Sunday school when I was only eight.
And every week you would say a prayer before the class would start;
And one day when you said that prayer, I asked Jesus in my heart."

Then another man stood before you.
He said, "Remember the time a missionary came to your church,
His pictures made you cry? You didn't have much money, but you gave it anyway;
Jesus took the gift you gave, that's why I'm here today."

Thank you for giving to the Lord!
I am a life that was changed.
Thank you for giving to the Lord!
I am so glad you gave!

One by one they came, as far as the eye could see,
Each life somehow touched by your generosity.
Sacrifices made, unnoticed on the earth,
In heaven now proclaimed.

I know up in heaven you're not supposed to cry,
But I am almost sure there were tears in your eyes;
As Jesus took your hand, you stood before the Lord:
He said, "My child, look around you, for great is your
reward!"[17]

Have no doubt. You will recognize all your loved ones and
others too!

Yours from the Other Side

&

Dear Child of God,

Yesterday I took a long walk through the woods, across
green meadows, and down past the cool waters of the River
of Life. I sat down on the bank to soak in the matchless beauty
of God's perfect creation and to reflect on the question you
asked about your grandparents.

They were such happy, hand-holding sweethearts for the
sixty years of their marriage. You asked, *What became of that
relationship? Was it buried in their graves?* This led you to
think about your own parents in light of your father's pro-

gressing illness. Then you brought it down to your own marriage. Because you just celebrated your twentieth anniversary, marriage in heaven suddenly seems very important to you. (By the way, happy anniversary!)

Of course you brought up the subject with your small group. Since you now know you'll recognize each other up here, you wondered what that means for marital relationships.

I'll see if I can help you. Let me start by saying that those who are happily married always hope and pray they'll still be married in heaven. And those who find themselves in a bad marriage hope and pray they won't be.

There are several important thoughts to keep in mind when dealing with this question. First of all, remember that marriage has always had a special place throughout Scripture as a symbol of our relationship with the Lord Jesus Christ. Those who committed their lives to Jesus are often referred to as His Bride and Jesus is referred to as the Bridegroom. In fact, the first glorious event that takes place after the Second Coming is called the Marriage Supper of the Lamb.[18] Still there will be no marriage or giving of marriage in heaven.[19] There are two reasons for this.

First, there is no exclusivity in heaven. The one thing you can say about marriage with absolute certainty is that it's exclusive. Your marriage vows are sacred, and you would never consider sharing your spouse with another person. You promised to love, honor, and cherish one another right up to the point of death. That's what sets marriage apart from other casual relationships. But in heaven there is no thought like, *you belong to me and I belong to you.*

The second thing to keep in mind when dealing with marriage in heaven is this: From the beginning God created the husband-wife relationship as a means to help and encourage each other in specific areas of responsibility on earth. Then He blessed it and set it apart from all other earthly relationships. He gave it as a physical and spiritual way of meeting one another's needs for intimacy and relationship. In heaven these needs are fully met in Christ. Therefore the need for an exclusive relationship with another person is gone. I realize this is one of those heavenly truths you'd prefer not to think about. I understand that response because it really is impossible for you to grasp this concept while on earth. God wants you to feel this way about your marriage. It's good and right. I can only assure you that the treasured love you hold in your heart is perfected in heaven. As a result, for the first time you'll understand what it means to be utterly free to love as God created you to love—something no one on earth has ever experienced.

Remember, you don't love someone just for the few years you live on earth. Don't ever forget that God is love. He created love. You'll discover complete joy and happiness in all of your relationships up here and experience a far deeper love and appreciation for one another. At last the image of God will be complete in your lives. You'll have new experiences of sharing, exploring the vast universes, skiing, boating, just being with family and friends—all in the loving presence of God.

The joy of heaven is that we all belong to the family of God. In fact you could call heaven the "great gathering place" because it is where Jesus said He would gather His beloved children from the four corners of the earth to be with Him.[20] Jesus has given you such a glorious picture of your reunion in heaven. It will be like the best Thanksgiving dinner you ever had with your family on earth. All your loved ones will be gathered around the table, laughing and eating delicious food. This is a glimpse into the wonderful fellowship you will enjoy at the banquet table of the Lord.

So while there is no marriage in heaven, you will someday be together with all your loved ones who have put their trust in Jesus. And what happy shouts and laughter will ring throughout the courts of heaven as you catch up on all the news, relate happy stories of memories past, and make exciting plans for things you will do and see together.

Thanks be to God!

Yours from the Other Side

CHAPTER 5
What Will We Do?

Dear Child of God,

Now that you have some idea of what you'll be like in heaven, we can move on to your other question: *What do we do in heaven?* When I lived on earth I often wondered the same thing. I couldn't begin to imagine what I'd do in heaven for eternity. It was one of those questions I quickly put out of my mind because the answer seemed so elusive and unknowable. But I'm glad you asked because I could identify with your apprehension and curiosity. I'm looking forward to sharing the answer with you in the next several letters. It's an absolutely joyful answer. Believe me, it's beyond your fondest expectation.

First of all, it's important to remember that heaven is a place where there's creative and challenging activity. I promise you, you'll not be lolling around on silken pillows eating chocolates for eternity! Nor will you become an eternal couch potato. You won't spend eternity strolling down flower-strewn streets of gold. Heaven is not a place where you "enter your eternal rest" and then do nothing.

It's true there will be times when you'll want to rest and be quiet. Some people worked so hard on earth that they simply want to rest quietly beside the Crystal Sea and be refreshed by the unique, eternal beauty that surrounds them. Up here we like to refer to it as "sacred idleness." You can sit and enjoy the incredible beauty of God's heaven. You can watch animals that were enemies on earth romping and resting together. You may just want to be still and know that, in the hushed silence, God is with you, enfolding you in peaceful solitude and covering you with His everlasting love. In the glory of His presence, you're clothed in God's boundless energy. You're continually refreshed, restored, and renewed. For this reason, you won't *need* to rest here because you'll never be weary or weak or tired in heaven. Up here you rest for the sheer pleasure of resting. Now isn't that cause for rejoicing?

Heaven isn't like anything you thought it would be. There are so many creative things you'll want to accomplish. And when you finish them, you'll have that good feeling of a job completed right. That's part of heaven you will never grow tired of—hearing God's joyful "well done." Yes, you will have much to do here, but it isn't called work or play, it's simply called *living!* You'll have an endless variety of fascinating responsibilities. As author Joseph Bayly aptly described it, heaven certainly isn't one long "Sunday afternoon nap."[1] In fact, maybe you'll manage a city or a village, or take care of one of the universes!

Remember, Adam and Eve had much work to do in the Garden of Eden. They cared for all the flowers, plants, trees, and vegetables. Adam named all the animals and with Eve he tended them. (Just naming all of them would have been a challenging task in itself.) And if that weren't enough, God put them in charge of the entire earth.[2] (Humankind hasn't done a very good job of caring for it.) They were also to take care of each other and any children they'd have (another sometimes neglected area on earth). But while Adam and Eve were in the garden, their work was absolutely fulfilling and not burdensome until they disobeyed God and ate from the tree of knowledge of good and evil.[3] Until then their joy was complete in the Lord. They had perfect fellowship with Him. They enjoyed long walks with God in the "cool of the day." They also enjoyed hearing Him say "well done" at the end of each day when they showed Him all they'd accomplished. Adam and Eve experienced unbroken happiness in their fellowship with one another and with the Lord God whom they adored and worshiped.

What God has waiting for you when you arrive here at His appointed time is even better than you can imagine. You too will have duties to share and tasks that will use all of your creative abilities. Heaven is where all your talents and abilities are perfected. They continue to develop in ways you never imagined possible. There are always new "hidden" talents for you to discover and learn to use for the glory of God, the blessing of others, and the inexpressible joy they will bring to you.

It will take several more letters to answer your question about what you'll do in heaven. I'm enjoying this process of helping you get a new perspective on all God has waiting for you here. It's going to be good, I promise you. More importantly, God promises you!

Yours from the Other Side

❧

Dear Child of God,

Have you ever gone to a library and longed to know what all the books said? That was always one of my dreams when I lived on earth. And not only to know what they said, but to be able to remember everything I read and put all that knowledge into practice. Well, guess what? You can do that in heaven!

We have the finest libraries you could ever imagine. They make the world-famous Bodleian Library in Oxford, England, which contains over three million books, look like the library at your neighborhood elementary school.

Remember, when God created you He planted within you a desire to study and learn. Here in heaven that desire is intensified. God gives you a deep hunger and thirst for knowledge of Himself, creation, science, and all of the other universes and planets. The knowledge you gain from your first five minutes in heaven opens your eyes to the unlimited access to knowledge God has waiting for you.[4]

You can begin to discover that knowledge when you study at heaven's finest universities. Classes are offered in every conceivable subject. History, mathematics, engineering, aeronautics, science, and interplanetary studies are all waiting to be discovered. There are art lessons available from the finest Christian artists. (Maybe your finished painting will hang in the place of honor in your home or in one of heaven's magnificent art galleries.) There are classes offered in every sport known, and as yet unknown to you. How would you like to take skiing lessons from one of the great Olympic ski instructors? There are ballet lessons from some of heaven's most accomplished dancers. Or you can study acting and perform in plays written by heaven's famous playwrights. I could write enough pages to fill an entire book about all the wonderful, challenging subjects there are to study and learn about. But this gives you a small idea of what you can look forward to.

There's so much to learn and so many ways to grow here in heaven. The best part of all is that there is time to study and develop this gift of wisdom that involves understanding all you have learned. In heaven all learning is stimulating and enjoyable—and you never have to worry about final exams! You can walk through the gardens of the universities and libraries and see small groups of people sitting on the lawn, excitedly sharing their latest thoughts and ideas of the wondrous mysteries they've just discovered. There are countless ways to use the knowledge you learn for the glory of God and the edification of others. On earth only the smallest part of the brain is used. In heaven it's used to the fullest. True knowledge is always creative, and God, the originator of all, has endless ways to use your knowledge. There are new books to write, new music to compose, new masterpieces of art to paint. Growing and learning is a continual process here in heaven. There's the constant joy of spiritual and intellectual growth, all done in the context of God's complete love and perfection. All knowledge is at your disposal.

You'll have the privilege of studying under some of the leading professors whose names are written in the Book of Life. Maybe you would like to study with C. S. Lewis, Eugene Peterson, or J. I. Packer. (These last two haven't arrived here yet.) Then there are Augustine, John Bunyan, and so many others. Or how would you like to study with Moses, Daniel, or David? Ruth, Esther, or Sarah? Or any of the other great Old Testament men and women of God you've read about? They're all here and looking forward to sharing with you. Think of listening to the disciples talk about their adventures and all they learned from the time of their first encounter with Jesus on the shores of Galilee. Then there's Paul, that brilliant apostle and writer of much of the New Testament.

But by far the most wonderful privilege of all will be sitting at the feet of Jesus and learning more and more about Him—your great Redeemer, Savior, and Lord. He'll share with you the great mysteries of all the universes. But the greatest mystery He'll ever explain is the mystery of why He went to Calvary and why He loves you so. All of the knowledge and wisdom of heaven is built upon the foundation of this priceless treasure—God's everlasting love for you.

Yours from the Other Side

Dear Child of God,

You wrote that your father always wanted to be a world-famous orchestra conductor. Well, based on my last letter about being able to learn new things in heaven, you can tell him that up here he can have his heart's desire. He'll be able to study under heaven's most distinguished conductors, and when he graduates, he'll be invited to direct the symphony orchestra at the Holy City Opera House. What an evening that will be. (Save me a seat on the front row!)

I'm glad you brought up the subject of music because it's such an important part of worship in heaven. You may remember that during Old Testament times the most blessed place for the Jewish people was the temple. They longed to be there. David said, "I'm asking GOD for one thing, only one thing: to live with him in his house my whole life long. I'll contemplate his beauty; I'll study at his feet."[5] The temple was the place where God lived among His people. If they wanted to be in His presence they went to the temple. It wasn't just a sacred place where they worshipped Him, but a place of total joy and delight. There was singing and dancing in the house of God. It was where musicians played instruments in praise.

Again read the exuberant words of David, "Sing to GOD a brand new song, praise him in the company of all who love him. . . . Let them praise his name in dance; strike up the band and make great music."[6] Do you sense the joy here? It's because the Lord God takes such delight in His people that we in turn are able to take delight in Him. And there's more! "Praise him with castanets and dance, praise him with banjo and flute; praise him with cymbals and a big bass drum, praise him with fiddles and mandolin. Let every living, breathing creature praise GOD! Hallelujah!"[7] (Isn't that enough to make you want to dance around your living room with praise and joy to your great King of kings and Lord of lords?)

But it gets even better! God tells us in Revelation that His true temple, His eternal dwelling place, is in heaven. And in this place there will be joyful music and songs of great praise. Wherever God is, there is always unspeakable joy filled with glory. If there was singing, dancing, and music of trumpets, fiddles, banjos, and flutes in the first temple in Jerusalem, just think what the triumphant music, sung and played by the saints (that's you and me!), will be like in heaven.

Heaven is permeated with indescribably beautiful music, and God Himself is the Master Musician. Think for a moment of some of your favorite music. Recall how it can sometimes sound like waves crashing against a rocky shore, rain gently caressing spring's earliest blooms, or a thunderstorm exploding at dawn. As moving as the music you like best is, it's still only a foretaste of what you'll hear in heaven where each note is alive with God's creativity and radiance. It won't take long to discover that "heaven will be a musician's paradise."[8]

You can attend concerts sung by celestial choirs in heaven's magnificent concert halls. There will be times when you thrill to the works of great composers who died with their names written in the Book of Life. There are musicians to compose the music, poets to write the words, choirs to perform, and audiences to fully appreciate and understand the magnificence of each movement. Sometimes the music is so powerfully majestic that it sounds like a thundering waterfall grander than Niagara in North America or Victoria in South Africa. One glorious new song after the other fills the air with adoration and praise.

Heaven is where you'll hear the same angels who appeared to the shepherds the night Jesus was born in a Bethlehem stable. That night the sky was aflame with brilliant stardust as the angels said, "Glory to God in the Highest!" To this day, that same refrain echoes throughout the portals of heaven and will continue to do so throughout all eternity.

And oh! Think about this: *You* will join all believers as they sing in heaven's choir. Just as one of the characteristics of living close to Jesus on earth is a singing heart, so it is up here. You'll praise God continually with your song. Think how Handel's "Hallelujah Chorus" thrills you when you hear it. Just imagine what it will sound like with thousands upon thousands of voices singing to the praise and glory of God's eternal majesty.

What will you do in heaven? You'll worship the Lord your God with every form of celestial music. You'll join the angels and the completed family of God in singing, "To him who sits on the throne and to the Lamb be praise and honor and glory and power for ever and ever!"[9]

In heaven your song will be an eternal hallelujah!

Yours from the Other Side

&

Dear Child of God,

Your most recent question touches the very heart of God. *What do the children do in heaven?* Every parent who has lost a child asks this question. It's so hard to imagine your children being safe when they're not with you anymore. Even years after your loss, you can be moved to tears by simple things like seeing one of your child's friends or hearing your child's name called out by a mother calling her own child.

When you asked me about the children in heaven, I picked up my notebooks and walked down the flower-lined streets of gold, past the gleaming cities, through the small villages nestled against the rolling hills, and across the wooded valley to the beautiful Meadow of Rainbows. I wanted to spend several days observing the most cherished treasures in heaven—the children. You wanted to know what they do here. Do they sit on a curb crying because they don't know anyone and miss their mommy and daddy? I wish I'd done this sooner because I can't begin to tell you the blessing and joy that washed over me as I journeyed through heaven. When I returned to my home several days later, I felt as though I'd been dusted with happiness. I'll attempt to give you an idea of what I saw and experienced.

First of all, let me assure you that each time a child dies, the angels bow their heads in silence because they know the child's arrival here has brought deep and lasting sorrow to the loved ones left behind on earth. Remember, death is the great enemy of God. Sickness and death are not from God but are the natural results of living in a fallen, sinful world. When a child dies, he or she is received in heaven most tenderly. Picture the angels carrying the little one from earth and placing him or her directly into the arms of Jesus.

And how does Jesus receive each child? In the same gentle, loving way He did when He walked the dusty roads of Galilee. No matter how many people needed Him, Jesus always stopped and took time to reach out and touch the little children. He drew them close and blessed them. They were the joy of His life on earth, and they remain the joy of His life here in heaven.

The difference is that in heaven children become all God created them to be. Think what that means! All of their potential—all of their creativity—is fully realized. Their ability to worship God and join the heavenly host in praising Him is theirs to enjoy forever. This is part of what happens to children when they die. All of this and so much more!

Just as children are treasures to parents on earth, they are to Jesus in heaven too. I'm sure you remember reading how He held a little child on His lap. He reminded the world that day that children are special blessings, that the kingdom of heaven is made up of His beloved children, and that each person on earth must become like a child if he or she wants to come to heaven.[10] What was Jesus saying? Did He want everyone to revert to childhood? Or was He teaching us that somehow we should retain the simple, uncomplicated attitude of a child? And what are children like? Children are born with a beautiful, loving, trusting, forgiving spirit. They have an exuberant joy of living and a simple trust in their parents. How different life would be if we were able to hold on to these basic characteristics throughout our lives.

But you asked, *what do the children do in heaven?* How I wish you could see them as I did when I walked through heaven these last few days. The first thing you might have noticed is that heaven is filled with their singing and laughter. They play together in grassy fields, catching bright-colored butterflies, giving them a quick kiss, and watching them fly away. In heaven, children can soar with the birds over a rainbow. Their laughter rings out like silver bells.

Small groups of children sometimes spread out on their tummies on the velvet grass, coloring pictures with crayons of iridescent colors only seen in heaven. During my long walk, I passed one little boy who was lying in a flower-covered meadow reading a book with his head resting on the back of a lion. A tiny lamb, pure and clean as snow, was curled up next to him. What a picture of total peace, security, and contentment! I saw the pleasure the animals bring to the children as they played together. Rosy-cheeked children were shouting merrily as they played hide-and-go-seek with baby kangaroos. Two little boys were taking a ride on the back of a graceful tiger. Another pair of adventuresome little girls were soaring through the cloudless sky on the wings of an eagle. Their hair was blowing straight out behind them as their joyous laughter rang through the pristine air. What a sight!

Are you surprised we have animals here in heaven? Why wouldn't there be? When God first created the human race, He put the animals under our protective care.[11] Animals are very special to God. The children are able to enjoy their playfulness without any trace of harm or danger just as God intended when He created them. Never forget that animals had a special place in the garden, they have a special place there on earth, and they have a special place here in heaven where you can enjoy them in complete safety forever.

Well, I have to tell you I came home with a singing heart and the absolute assurance that the children in heaven are joyfully cared for and tenderly loved by Jesus, the angels, and their many friends. As part of God's family, they're never sad or lonely. They love their family on earth but now with an intense, perfected love that is eternal. And one day, as they are swinging on the garden gate, they will see their parents and other loved ones who accepted God's gift of forgiveness step over the border into heaven.

Yours from the Other Side

&

Dear Child of God,

Thank you for telling me about the lovely dinner party you had recently with your study group. I could picture all of you enjoying your favorite dishes, sitting around the table decorated with fresh flowers and the warm glow of candlelight. What fellowship! I enjoyed reading about your conversation when you each shared some of the things you've learned about heaven in your study together. And then you went around the table and told the story of when you first met Jesus. Now that's a conversation I'd have liked to have been a part of! It's always interesting how each story is so different, yet so similar. Jesus always meets us individually, where we are, at that particular time of life. And from that point on, life is never the same. Your personal faith journey is one of the first things you'll share with everyone up here. "How did you meet Jesus?" is heard all the time, and no one ever grows weary of listening to the answer.

I can understand why no one wanted to go home! You wondered if you'll have times like that in heaven. If you think you enjoy candlelight dinners with your friends and loved ones there on earth, just wait until you get here! I promise you, what you experienced last night is just a minuscule glimpse into the joy awaiting you. You were right when you kept saying, "This is just like a little bit of heaven!"

Here, you'll discover endless creative ways to fix delicious gourmet dinners for your current friends and many new ones. There will be good food and fellowship, joyful laughter, worship, and praise. I've already mentioned the great Marriage Supper of the Lamb when God calls all of His children home.[12] It will be the greatest of all celebrations—the best food, perfect fellowship, joyful laughter, reverent worship, and pure praise. You won't want to miss it! And that's just the beginning. One of the nice things about eating up here is that you eat for pure enjoyment, not because you need to.

I know, when you think about eating in heaven you wonder who is going to grow the food, prepare the meal, and do the dishes. That's what I call a good, healthy, earthly question! That might seem like a logical question right now because you see all those tasks as work or even drudgery. Up here things are done very differently, and while everyone is busy, no one feels burdened. It isn't even necessary to *cook* heavenly food! Of course you can if you want to. Once you get here, you'll wonder why such a question ever occurred to you.

Oh! Another thing you'll like knowing is that you'll never get fat or worry about cholesterol. How's that for a happy thought? In fact, you can eat all the chocolate-covered donuts, ice cream bars, or cookies you want. (I can imagine you saying, "Now that's what I call heaven!")

But back to the question of what you'll *do* in heaven. Just remember that heaven is a place where your love and knowledge for one another and for the Lord Jesus will continue to grow. You'll visit each other in your homes, take long walks together, work together, and serve together. All for the glory of God. Everything you do will be done in the context of His honor and glory.

You'll never tire of inviting people like David over and listening to their latest songs of praise to the Lord. Or how about having Mary over to find out what she thought when the angel told her she was pregnant and would give birth to the Son of God? Then there's Jonah. He's always ready to tell how he felt when he spent three days inside the big fish that God had specially prepared for the occasion.[13] He'll be happy to share with you all God taught him.

Think of the honor of having dinner with some of the martyrs—those who were sawed in half, made into human torches for games in the Roman Coliseum, or killed in other horrible ways because of their faith in Christ. They chose to die rather than deny their love for Jesus Christ.

Even now on earth, thousands of people are suffering untold agony and death for Christ. Someday you'll have the privilege of hearing their stories of courage and God's provision. Like me, you'll be humbled by their faith. (Did you know there have been more martyrs in the twentieth century alone than in all the history of the world?)

These martyrs have a special place here in heaven. Jesus often accompanies them when they go out to share their story, and when He does, He never sits down while they speak. He stands out of deep respect and honor for all they endured for His name's sake.

Such is our great King of kings and Lord of lords!

Just think, part of what you'll do in heaven is get acquainted with the rest of your family of God.

Yours from the Other Side

&

Dear Child of God,

Throughout my letters, I've mentioned so many things we do here in heaven. Everything we do here is a form of worship. That's because all of heaven is filled with worship and thanksgiving to God. Joyful praise comes as naturally to us as breathing did on earth. We don't divide our life here into small compartments of work, study, play, fellowship, fun, or worship. That's something people do on earth. Up here, whether we're working, playing, sharing a meal, praising God, laughing, having fun, or simply sitting at the feet of Jesus, we do all to the praise and honor of our majestic Lord and Savior. It truly is the way J. I. Packer described it, "He made us with the intention that He and we might walk together in a love relationship."[14] You can enjoy your fellowship with Jesus up here in many ways, as well as having good times with family and friends (both new and old). But remember, as you read this letter, everything you do here will be done in the context of praise and worship to God.

So today, I want to list some of the happy activities you can take part in here in heaven. Some of the strange ideas people on earth have about heaven never cease to amaze me. (Of course, I had a lot of those same ideas before I got here!) I'm glad I've been able to give you a new perspective. Thank you for asking me to clear up one of the points I made in a recent letter. When I said heaven is a place of total perfection I didn't mean it was a place of total completion, where all creation is over and done with.

Nothing could be farther from the truth. Remember, God is the Creator of all. The first words in the Bible are "In the beginning God created." The apostle John said that all creation took place through Him. In Colossians, Paul states that all things were made by Him.[15] To create is God's nature — part of His very essence. This truth is found throughout Scripture. When God finished creating the world and the human race, He didn't just stop. Believe me, God isn't sitting in an easy chair, scratching His head, and wondering if there's anything left for Him to do! Creation and creativity is ongoing. God isn't frozen in place and neither is heaven. And God's people are definitely not the "frozen chosen"! Heaven is not where everyone turns into a piece of petrified wood the moment they arrive. I'm glad you brought this up. I hope this letter will reinforce the truth that all of heaven is alive with creativity, action, joy, worship, and adoration.

I want to focus on the pure enjoyment of heaven. As always I'll use earthly examples to express the heavenly recreation you'll delight in. These letters are written so you can have a bird's-eye view into the quality of life here. At times I must use symbols from earth to describe the activities of heaven. But try to picture yourself doing all of the things I'm going to mention and then imagine how you'd feel doing each one. This will give you some idea of how awe-inspiring and delightful life in heaven really is.

Begin by picturing yourself taking a walk with Abraham or Isaiah. Can you imagine what that would be like? What would you talk about? Or how about sitting in a garden gazebo with Mary, the mother of Jesus, and listening to the many stories she has to tell. Can you imagine skiing one of heaven's highest peaks alongside Jesus, shouting with laughter all the way down? Can you picture Jesus having a good time? He invented fun and laughter you know! And as the author of happiness, He takes delight in being happy.

Picture heaven as a place where you have time to develop new friendships and renew old ones. (There's even time to complete a conversation up here!) Imagine sitting on your deck with friends, visiting and sharing as long as you want because no one is in a hurry. Perhaps there are fireflies dancing across your lawn, sprinkling stardust through the warm, scented air.

Or picture:

◆ Taking a cruise on a floating palace across one of heaven's vast oceans or drifting lazily on the Crystal Sea. There's no such thing as motion sickness here!

◆ Hiking one of heaven's majestic mountains, past aquamarine glaciers, with the cold, fresh air brushing your face and painting roses on your cheeks. You needn't fear frostbite or broken bones because there's no pain or suffering in heaven.

◆ Bicycling throughout the many hills and valleys, around one of the many lakes. You can ride as long and hard as you like and never get tired.

◆ Taking a rocket ship safari over and around all of God's new creation, discovering more and more about Him and His creativity.

◆ Having a picnic with friends (or alone if you prefer) and sitting quietly on a soft carpet of grass and wildflowers free from all insect stings and spider bites.

◆ Enjoying an afternoon of tennis, golf, or one of the many other heavenly sports in settings so spectacular it'll be hard to concentrate on the ball.

◆ Diving deep into the sea with myriad colorful fish and ocean plants all around you. Imagine never worrying about surfacing too fast and getting the bends.

Perhaps you will want to:

♦ Dance with joy
♦ Paint Jesus' portrait
♦ Write stories of God's goodness
♦ Compose music for celestial choirs
♦ Build homes fit for angels
♦ Design eternal furniture

Imagine:

♦ Singing harmony with birds
♦ Petting a tiger cub
♦ Chasing (and catching) a rainbow
♦ Closing your eyes and breathing in the quiet eternal beauty
♦ Drinking from the River of Life alongside a doe with soft black eyes
♦ Strolling a beach and collecting one of every kind of seashell
♦ Sitting on a silver seashore with Jesus enjoying the quiet beauty

You'll be able to do all this—and so much more—in heaven. I'm sure you noticed I could only use earthly language and images. Believe me, I feel utterly limited. (A new feeling for me up here!) Perhaps you can begin to realize that heaven is far beyond your experience on earth.

Now there's one thing I can tell you that you can understand at least in part. Someday you will walk the streets of heaven with Jesus by your side. You'll revel in the quiet beauty of God's creation as you share your thoughts and feelings together. You'll begin to understand that heaven is where all of life — including you — is one song of eternal, joyful praise to the Lord. You'll discover that the greatest goal anyone on earth can ever have is to know God and to enjoy Him forever. To know Him as the majestic, all-powerful, all-wise God. To know Him perfectly as "the LORD [who] reigns, he is robed in majesty."[16] God is a personal God of infinite love and compassion and the God of infinite majesty and greatness. As J. I. Packer wrote, "The word majesty when applied to God is always a declaration of his greatness and an invitation to worship."[17]

Heaven is where that invitation is fully accepted and God is worshipped in all His radiant splendor and glory as the great Creator of all, as the Alpha and the Omega, the beginning and the end, as the One who spoke and all creation came into being. As God Almighty. Your eternal song up here will be "Great is the LORD and most worthy of praise."[18] When you catch a glimpse of the greatness and majesty of God, you will fall on your knees and sing with a full heart,

> "Holy, holy, holy
> is the Lord God Almighty,
> who was, and is, and is to come."[19]

Yours from the Other Side

℘

Dear Child of God,

Today it's my turn to ask questions. As you read these letters, is your image of God beginning to change? In what way? As you reflect on the reality of heaven, how has His character come into clearer focus for you? Are you leaving your earthly perspective behind as you gain new insights about heaven? These are all questions you may want to reflect on before you get my next letter. Perhaps you'll even want to discuss them in your small-group Bible study.

As a result of having a better understanding of what you'll do in heaven, do you feel you are coming to know God more intimately? I wonder how you see Him today in light of the glory of heaven. Do you see Him as the loving, omnipotent, holy, righteous God of the Bible? Do you see Him, as some do, as the great stern judge just waiting to strike you with the "ugly stick" the minute you do something wrong? How would you describe God to your children? Do you ever see Him as joyful, smiling, and happy? Can you imagine Him laughing heartily? Can you picture Him hiking up one of the beautiful mountains He created? Can you see Him sitting in a meadow with you and a group of friends, holding you in rapt attention as He relates an account of Creation or some other biblical event? Or do you only see Him sitting on a marble throne throughout eternity, listening to endless choirs singing praises to Him? Do you see Him as the great giver of joy—because He *is* joy? Do you see Him as the One who loves you with an everlasting love—because He *is* love?

Can you picture Jesus sitting on the terrace of your heavenly home with you? What do you think He'd say? Can you imagine what it will be like to ask Him all the questions you have as you journey through life?

Remember, heaven is a place where you are fully alive. You'll have perfect communication with Jesus because there won't be any sin standing in the way. You'll see Him face to face—this great Lord and Savior. Although you can't see Him on earth, you love Him and have entrusted your eternal life to Him. This is the Jesus you'll know fully in heaven. Because of Him, God is your loving heavenly Father and you're His dearly loved child.

As beautiful and wonderful as the physical heaven is, nothing will ever compare with the blessed joy of just being with Jesus! You'll be immersed in His love for you and worship Him with holy praise, for you shall see Him as He is.[20]

At last you will understand what the Psalmist meant when he said, "You will fill me with joy in your presence, with eternal pleasure at your right hand."[21] Heaven is where you experience the eternal joy of the Lord. It is:

Where you will see Jesus,
Where you will be with Him,
And where He will be with you forever.

All this, and so much more, is what you'll do in heaven.

Yours from the Other Side

CHAPTER 6
Until We Get There

Dear Child of God,

You asked an important question that has troubled people down through the centuries: *If heaven is so wonderful, why don't I want to go there today?* Believe me, you're not the first person to struggle with this question. I remember when I lived on earth, I used to pray, "Please Lord, let me get married first." After that, I wanted to have children. Then I wanted to see them graduate from college. And what parent wants to miss a child's wedding? Of course, after that you have to see your grandchildren. When all the grandchildren are born, you still don't want to go to heaven because you want to enjoy "the golden years" with your spouse or close friends.

No matter how wonderful heaven is, you really aren't too anxious to come here any time soon. You don't want to leave your family and friends who still need you; you have responsibilities you need to take care of; you have more dreams and plans to carry out. Very few people would say they want to go to heaven today unless they're elderly, in pain, or involved in a tragic situation. Of course, if most of their loved ones are already here in heaven, then they're more anxious to come.

Don't you see? The point of all this is that you're *supposed* to feel this way. God created you to feel this way. Your life is one of God's most precious gifts to you. He gave it to you to enjoy, to have fellowship with Him, and to experience all the good things He has planned for you. He expects you to protect and care for your life. When you give a gift to someone, you want them to enjoy it. God feels the same way. He created you to be an image bearer of Himself. That means you're a thinking, moral, rational being with an intense desire to live. It's the most natural thing for you to want to continue living. Never forget that life (and every good thing in it) is from God. Every part of it—from the daily joys to the conflicts and tensions everyone faces from time to time, from the ecstasy of new love to the pain of separation, from the opportunities and successes to the disappointments and failures—comes through God's filter of love. God has placed a zest for life in your heart for right now and for all eternity.

Yes, you have a longing in your heart for Jesus, but you also have an equal longing to stay on earth and finish the course He's planned for you. Writing to new believers in Philippi, Paul felt the same way: "I am torn between the two: I desire to depart and be with Christ, which is better by far; but it is more necessary for you that I remain in the body."[1] This is God's will. At the right time in your life, God begins to prepare your heart for heaven. Most people over age eighty would probably say they're ready to go today. They find their thoughts turning more and more to Jesus and their heavenly home. God designed this natural progression. Young people diagnosed with terminal illnesses often begin to talk about being with Jesus even before their parents or doctors have explained how ill they are. God in His grace and wisdom gives them a longing for heaven.

For now, God has given you the gift of life to enjoy, to

learn how to live and how to give, how to love and how to serve Him and those around you. He requires you to take care of this priceless gift and intends for you to enjoy and use each day He permits you to live on earth for His glory.

Your physical life and your eternal life are to be cherished equally as gifts from God. If you're not longing to come to heaven today, it's because God has too many things for you to do for Him right where you are.

Enjoy doing them!

Yours from the Other Side

❧

Dear Child of God,

I was glad to hear you've taken some time to think about my last letter. I want to assure you that God doesn't want you walking around earth carrying a huge bundle of guilt just because you don't want to come to heaven yet. That's what He calls "self-imposed guilt," which, by the way, is a good name because it definitely doesn't come from Him.

I was interested to learn that when you spent time in God's Word and in prayer, you reached your own answer to your question, *If heaven is so wonderful, why don't I want to go there now?* It's good to grapple with these questions and let God reveal His truth to you. You reached the right conclusion. God gave you dreams of places to go and things to do on earth. He wants you to enjoy the beautiful world

He made. He expects you to complete your task of caring for those He's placed in your care. He understands it's difficult to be excited about a place you've never seen and have trouble even imagining. I hope you carry through on your decision to never feel guilty again because of your joy in living.

One of the results of walking close to Jesus each day is joy. Let me share with you something I continue to learn up here. Jesus is pleased each time you share in His joy. Have you ever stopped to think of the continual suffering and sorrow He sees each day there on earth? He witnesses the unending inhumanity people show each other. He observes the incessant hate and evil that runs rampant throughout the earth. He's grieved by the constant devastation of sin. Believe me, when God sees you content and happy, He's delighted.

Joy is not just reserved for heaven. It's yours on earth whenever you're in His presence. What are some of the things that bring you into His presence?

- ◆ Knowing you belong to Jesus
- ◆ Reflecting on His gift of life
- ◆ Enjoying the loving relationships He's sent your way
- ◆ Appreciating the work He's given you to do there on earth
- ◆ Serving Him at home, at work, at school, and at play
- ◆ Walking close to Jesus a moment at a time
- ◆ Sharing your life with Him in prayer each day
- ◆ Feeding on the Word of God through the reading and studying of Scripture

- Accomplishing the mission He's called you to
- Sharing the love of Jesus with your family, neighbors, fellow workers, friends at school, or anyone you meet
- Letting your faith in God show before all you meet so they may see your good works and glorify your Father who is in heaven[2]

God has placed the desire for life deep within your heart. Enjoy it. And then, hear His quiet whisper, "Thank you for your joy."

Yours from the Other Side

❧

Dear Child of God,

Thank you for reminding me of that tired expression that has been around for centuries: "Don't become so heavenly minded that you're no earthly good." Talk about twisting the truth! I know that type of thinking too often kept me from focusing on heaven when I lived on earth. And I'm confident it continues to keep people from wanting to become too aware of heaven. I remember I didn't want to be one of those "heavenly minded" people who walked around with a pious, ethereal expression and didn't care much about what happened around them.

This attitude can be insidious and destructive. It has kept theologians from preaching about heaven, authors from writing about heaven, and people from embracing the reality of heaven. As a result, much of the wonder and joy that comes from living with heaven in view is lost. This opens the door to all kinds of counterfeit ideas and heresies.

It's always helpful to remember what heresies are because they're so prevalent today. A heresy is a distortion of the truth. It always includes enough truth to make it acceptable and enough error to lead people astray. And that's what sometimes happens regarding heaven. Actually there *is* a danger of becoming so heavenly minded you really are of no earthly good. When this happens, you neglect the people God has placed under your care. You fail to accomplish the work God has called you to and miss out on fulfilling His plan for you on earth. On the other hand, this error comes from accepting the lie that you will be of *no* earthly good if you become more heavenly minded. Believe me, nothing could be further from the truth. In fact, the more you focus on heaven, the more earthly good you'll want to become. When you live with heaven in view, you become sensitive and receptive to the opportunities God gives you on earth. When your mind is centered on Jesus and heaven, you discover a greater desire to share God's love with others. A new awareness of the everlasting glory of heaven brings a deeper understanding of God's love for you and the lost and dying world that surrounds you.

As you become more heavenly focused, praise wells up within your heart. Suddenly you have a deep desire to praise God throughout the day. You discover it's totally natural to sing His praises while working at home, driving in the car, worshiping at church, and even visiting with friends. God's praise tumbles from your lips. As a result every semblance of a grumbling attitude disappears. (There's no way you can be a grumbling, grateful Christian.) This makes you easier to live with and everyone around you happier. Soon a spirit of joyful thanksgiving takes root at the center of your being. You begin to realize that your life has received a touch from heaven. You learn to praise God every morning and thank Him for His faithfulness every night. Life will never be the same when you live with heaven in view.

Don't fear becoming more heavenly minded as long as you continue to ask God how a clearer view of heaven can make you *more* effective—more earthly good.

Yours from the Other Side

❧

Dear Child of God,

I'm glad you took me up on my challenge to begin living each day with heaven in view by singing praise songs out loud at home. Good for you! I had to chuckle when you said your whole family was startled when they heard you singing in the shower. I knew you'd understand what I was saying in my last letter. I'm not surprised that a spirit of joy seems to permeate the entire house just because you sing. Praise is contagious, you know! Believe me, this is just the beginning of a new way of living for you. You're in for some great blessings and challenging adventures. I'm looking forward to sharing them with you.

I enjoyed hearing about your recent trip to the art museum. Sometimes it's nice to do things like that by yourself. There's something special about being in a museum filled with great masterpieces. Being surrounded by such beautiful works can quiet the mind. That was a good description you shared of sitting for nearly an hour in front of Monet's *Garden*. I could almost feel the stillness of the misty blue air and see the flowers caressed by the summer breeze. I understand how you felt in the midst of such intense beauty. I imagine it seemed as if you were right there in the middle of the garden where all was steeped in peace.

What a magical experience for you. For one shining moment you were totally lost in the wonder of the painting. When you longed to step over the picture frame into the garden, you caught a brief glimpse of what coming to heaven is like. Only Monet's *Garden* is just a picture. Heaven is real. Reluctantly you had to imagine yourself stepping back across the frame and into reality again. You won't have to do that in heaven. That's why you left the museum with a deep, unsettled yearning. It was a longing in your heart for Jesus and the reality of heaven. Maybe for the first time, you understood that the beauty of God's creation in the world is a mere reflection of heaven. C. S. Lewis explained that these reflections "are only the scent of a flower we have not found, the echo of a time we have not heard, news from a country we have never visited."[3]

Listen, even in your fallen, indifferent world God continues to whisper from generation to generation the truth of heaven through the majesty of His creation. It stands as a permanent signpost pointing you to Jesus and your eternal home.

As you become more heavenly minded, you'll start to see everything in a new light. Suddenly you become aware of the startling perfection of a rose or the quietness of falling snow. You hear with new ears the haunting call of the loon as it soars through the stormy sky or the crisp chiming of a church bell as it echoes back and forth across the countryside. You feel the surge of joy that rushes over you each time you see a majestic snow-covered mountain or smell the pungent fragrance of the golden autumn leaves etched against a brilliant blue sky. You listen to the laughing streams, witness the sparkling blue gleam of the river, and glory in the rose-pink clouds of a fading sunset or the soft colors of a rainbow. All this (and all creation) is just a shadow of the wonder that is awaiting you in heaven.

Like the sunbeam is to the sun, so the earthly creation is to heaven. Creation is God's imprint of heaven throughout all the earth.

Yours from the Other Side

CHAPTER SEVEN

Eternity in Our Hearts

Dear Child of God,

This letter will be one of the more challenging ones I'll write because it deals with the concept of eternity. You know, you're the one who brought it up when you told me about your first experience with eternity at the tender age of ten. It was an interesting story, and I appreciate your sharing it with me. I'd like to make a couple of comments as I go through it with you.

You wrote how your mother had tucked you in bed, kissed you goodnight, and closed your bedroom door, leaving you alone in the darkness. For some strange reason, you began to think about eternity for the first time in your life. You wondered, *How long is forever?* What a big thought for such a little person! Of course, the subject was too huge and even terrifying for a ten-year-old to grapple with. Suddenly you felt a cold fear that sent you racing down the stairs to the safety of the living room where your parents sat reading. What a smart thing to do. Then you snuggled close to your mother and sobbed uncontrollably. You knew you felt afraid, but couldn't find the words to explain why. That was even scarier. For a moment you stood at the edge of eternity and couldn't bear its mystery and vastness. How could you? To think of living forever was far beyond your ability to comprehend. (After all, it was still hard for you to think very far beyond your next birthday or grade in school.)

Your mother knew just what to do. She sensed you'd experienced a terror you couldn't put into words, so she just held you close and rocked you back and forth until you stopped crying. (Aren't mothers wonderful?) Once you calmed down, she dried your tears and gave you a handful of salted peanuts before taking you back to bed.

As I think about your story, I'm sure you're absolutely right. It doesn't matter how young or old you are, if you think about eternity too long, you become totally overwhelmed. That's because eternity and everlasting life are such difficult concepts to grasp. My advice is, don't even try. You can never fully understand the meaning of those words as long as you live on earth. You have no frame of reference to go by. Everything you know has a starting and an ending time. Eternity doesn't. It's not a hundred million years. It's not even a circle with no beginning or end, as some theologians have tried to explain it. Neither is it some vague, long straight line that trails off into infinity.

Eternity is a completely different dimension from time. I hesitate to say it, but I agree with you: Eternity is incomprehensible for people on earth. Yet it's written on the pages of the Bible, and God has written it on the pages of your life. It's one of those things Scripture says you now see through a glass darkly but one day will be made crystal clear.[1]

Eternity exists in heaven. Now that I'm here, I understand it. And once you're here, you will too. Until then you can run to the Lord when you feel afraid about living forever. He'll comfort you just like your mom comforted you many years ago.

I hope my next letter will take away more of your concern.

Yours from the Other Side

ॐ

Dear Child of God,

You raised an interesting question at the end of your last letter: *Where does belief in life after death come from?* That question suggests you've noticed this belief is a common thread of truth woven throughout the history of civilization.

I remember going to Nepal when I lived on earth. While there I visited the city of Kathmandu. In the center of the city, surrounded by the Himalayan Mountains, stood the monumental Tibetan Stupa where the Buddhist *lamaseries* lived and worshiped. Inside, the air was heavy with incense. A group of monks sat on the floor in lotus position, chanting in an eerie continuous monotone that signified unending life—a belief in life after death. Since then I've learned that no matter where you go in the world—from the most modern cities to the deepest jungles, from the highest educated statesmen to the most backward tribes, from the heights of knowledge to the most primitive forms of witchcraft—you find a system of belief in life after death.

Cicero, the Roman philosopher, stated that even though he couldn't explain it, he found that all people believed in some form of future existence. Saint Augustine, a brilliant fourth-century theologian, referred to it as a "restless heart." Well-known author Charles Kingsley called it a "divine discontent." And author and theologian Eugene Peterson said that down through the centuries the human race has "given more attention and concern to divinity than to all their other concerns put together: food, housing, clothing, pleasure, work, family, whatever."[2] Those philosophers or intellectuals who don't accept this premise all come to the same conclusion: Life on the planet earth has no meaning if this is all there is. (Now that's what I call a dismal conclusion!)

Listen, if life on the planet earth is all there is, why spend years working? Why go to the jungle to teach people to read? Why do scientific research to create a new medicine to ease suffering or prolong life? Why paint a masterpiece or compose a symphony? Why shut yourself up in isolation to write a book? Why do anything for anybody? Why, if this life is all there is? Have you wondered about this? Has anyone ever asked you these questions? Maybe it was a student or a colleague at work, a neighbor, a friend, a child. I'm sure you've had discussions about this at some time during your life. If you haven't, believe me, you will! To wonder about these things is the beginning of knowledge. To seek answers to serious questions like these is the beginning of wisdom.

The answer, of course, rests with God. Just as He placed His imprint on the created world, He "planted eternity in our hearts" when He created us.[3] This truth lies at the very core of our existence. This treasure, this seed of eternity in your heart and mine, is part of the image of God implanted into every human being. All the good done in the world—works of art, scientific inventions, medical advances, kind and loving acts—springs from the small seed of eternity placed there by God. Even in the blackest moments or most difficult times of life, this tiny jewel is present within each person. This speck of eternity is the motivating factor behind all human good. And this is why there continues to be a universal belief in life after death. It's the starting point for everyone.

Yes—God planted eternity in your heart.

Yes—this truth lies at the very core of your existence.

Yes—it is the road sign pointing you to your eternal home.

Yours from the Other Side

❧

Dear Child of God,

Thanks for the prompt reply to my last letter. I loved the story of your eighty-five-year-old grandfather who told you he didn't feel a day over twenty-five! Don't you see? He caught the picture. The soul is ageless—it's eternal. On his seventieth birthday Victor Hugo expressed the same feeling when he said, "Winter is on my head, and eternal spring is in my heart."[4] The reason these men could say these things in all truth is because when God created them (and you), He breathed into them the breath of eternal life. *Your soul never grows old.* The real you remains the same regardless of how long you live on earth or how many wrinkles you get. At some point your physical body may not move as quickly as it used to, your eyes may grow dim, and your ears may not hear as well. You'll probably experience many aches and pains before your journey through life is complete. But listen to this: Your soul, the real you, never grows old, never dies. It is totally separate from your physical body. Another way to put it is to say you're an eternal soul living in a temporary body.

We've talked about it before. The human body is in a constant state of change. Each passing moment you lose countless skin cells, strands of hair, and many microscopic parts because your cells are always replacing themselves. This is a baffling scientific fact. You have a different body today than you did when you were five. And should you live many more years, your body will be completely unlike it is today. We are truly "fearfully and wonderfully made" as the Psalmist tells us.[5]

Your earthly body is captive to space and time and their effects, but your soul isn't. The Bible has an interesting way of explaining this. It says your body is like a tent that is taken down and folded away. It's like a garment. You take one garment off and exchange it for *life.* You get a totally new, incorruptible body.[6] Now that's something to rejoice about!

Your grandfather felt like a young man on the inside—where his soul lived—even though his body was old, wrinkled, and weak. When he died he discarded his old "tent." In heaven his eternal spirit took up residence in a new, improved body that will never wear out or need mending.

One of the old Masters depicted this awesome truth by

painting a picture of a very old man who had died. Behind him was God holding a laughing child in His arms. That's it!

Yours from the Other Side

⅋

Dear Child of God,

Well, have you caught your breath yet from our brief preview of eternity? I trust the thoughts I shared were helpful. One more issue important to eternity is the subject of time. Because our lives on earth are broken into segments measured by time, it's hard to imagine a timeless world.

I remember how my life on earth seemed controlled by clocks, calendars, and endless schedules. I was happy when I arrived here to learn there is no time. You can't imagine the freedom this brings. I know it's difficult to understand but the truth is, there simply isn't any time as you know it. I've been using the word *day* in my letters even though in heaven there is no day or night like you know them. There aren't any grandfather clocks, sounds of steeple bells ringing out the hour through the heavenly air, or even wristwatches. Best of all, no alarm clocks will pierce your morning dreams. How does that sound to you?

When I think of the way you live down there, I find myself saying over and over, "Thank you, Jesus, that I am here with You." I think of how you rush around, dashing frantically from one appointment to another. Sometimes I get out of breath just thinking about all the places you have to go and people you must see. I'm reminded of the poem my mother hung by our front door when I was growing up. Maybe you've seen it:

> Said the robin to the sparrow,
> "I should really like to know
> Why those anxious human beings
> Rush about and worry so."

> Said the sparrow to the robin,
> "Friend I think that it must be
> That they have no heavenly father
> Such as cares for you and me."[7]

God often used that little poem to remind me to slow down.

Time is such an impossible thing to control. It seems to work against you throughout your life. There are times when you want to speed it up, like shortly before your wedding day. Remember how slowly time seemed to pass in the weeks preceding it? You were sure time had come to a complete standstill and that your big day would never arrive. Then as you got older, you wanted time to slow down so your children wouldn't grow up so quickly.

I know you sometimes find yourself wishing you had more than one life so you could accomplish more of your dreams. That's part of the continual struggle with time. God gave each person just one life to live on earth. And He expects us to make our life count and to redeem the time. You mentioned you'd like to start an orphanage in India or teach the

Bible in Russia or work in a hospital in Africa. You wish there was more time to develop friendships with the people you meet. You'd like to have more time to spend with your family, to read a book, or just to sit on the patio and watch the clouds sail by. But the deepest prayer of your heart, I know, is to have more time to pray and to study God's Word. From your letter I sense your deep longing to be close to Jesus and to share His love with others.

It might be helpful to remember that Jesus understands what it's like to live in time and space and history. He lived within the limits of time when He was on earth. He often spoke of the fact that His time had not yet come. He was referring to the completion of time. Jesus tells us that His Second Coming will bring the consummation of all time. Actually, it should be a great comfort to you to know that someday time will be no more. Heaven is a place completely untouched by time. It's where time and eternity are united.

For now if you'd feel better about having time in heaven, I understand. Just think of it as heavenly time and go on from there. When J. R. R. Tolkien wrote of heaven in *The Lord of the Rings*, he said, "Time doesn't seem to pass here; it just is. A remarkable place altogether." Just imagine never having to hurry again!

Yours from the Other Side

CHAPTER EIGHT
The Problem of Pain and Suffering

Dear Child of God,

You recently asked some serious questions about suffering and death. I know this is a tender spot in your life right now as you face the coming death of your father. Please know how sorry I am for you and your mother as you go through this time of sorrow and loss. I want you to know I'm here to help you in any way I can. Your questions were direct and honest, and I'll do my best to answer them.

It's true that death is a trauma each person faces at some point during his or her journey through life. When you're faced with the death of a loved one, it's natural to ask the questions you did: *Is there really life after death or is life as fleeting as a flash of lightning that streaks across the sky and disappears into nothingness? Does life with all its wonder, love, and friendships stop at death?* I understood when you said that in your heart you know the answers to these questions, but the thought of being separated from your father raises all kinds of doubts. That too is normal. Read through the Psalms and list all the questions David asked during times of sorrow or loss in his life. Here are a few to get you started:

◆ Psalm 6:3: David was in such anguish he asked God, "How long, O LORD, how long?"

◆ Psalm 10:1: Sometimes God seems far away in the midst of our sorrow and we ask with David, "Why, O LORD, do you stand far off? Why do you hide yourself in times of trouble?"

◆ Psalm 22:1: When under unprovoked enemy attack, David cried, "My God, my God, why have you forsaken me? Why are you so far . . . from the words of my groaning?"

I know you can identify with these and other honest questions David asked. We all can. God has given us these passages and the rest of His Word to equip and encourage us on our way home to Him.

We know for every birth, there will be a death. What a vast difference there is between these two events. The first is greeted with great celebration, the other with great sorrow. And the way you cope with the death of your father will depend upon your definition of death. Since your questions about suffering and death are two distinct questions, I thought it would be helpful to deal with them separately.

In this letter I'll deal with your question about suffering—one that's been asked by every generation of humankind: *If God is a God of love, why does He allow so much sickness and suffering on earth?* I wish my answer could resound throughout the world: Suffering and sickness are not from God! They're from the Devil. When God created the world it was perfect but had the potential for evil. Sin and death entered the world as the result of the Fall, when people first disobeyed God. Sickness, pain, suffering, and death are not from God and never could be, just as truth, beauty, and good-ness could never come from the Devil. If you say God causes sickness and death, then you must say He is the author of evil, and that would be completely contrary to His character.

If sickness were *caused* by God, why go to the doctor or take medicine? If sickness were *from* God, doesn't it follow that even taking an aspirin would be an act of rebellion? God has provided medicine for the benefit of the human race. New discoveries are found almost daily. They're God's gifts to you for health and healing and should be used with a thankful heart.

Furthermore, if sickness and disease were from God, why would anyone want to be a doctor or a nurse? That would be working against the very sickness God supposedly sent. But visit almost any hospital throughout the world and see how God uses dedicated doctors and nurses to bring His love and care to the suffering. Remember, Jesus was called the Great Physician. He spent much of His ministry on earth healing people. God is against sickness in the same way He's against sin and death.

I've seen how God can take what Satan meant for harm and evil and use it for good. I'm sure you have too. Sickness has often been used to bring a person into God's family. I have a friend here in heaven who wandered down the wrong road of life while on earth until God used sickness to set her back on the right track. Sometimes He uses suffering to help a person get his or her priorities back in order. When my uncle was president of a manufacturing business, he always arrived home late for dinner, bringing a bulging briefcase with him. He rarely took a vacation and had no time for his family. His life was filled with constant coming and going until he had a heart attack. You couldn't say it came from God or the Devil. It came from the hectic pace of his stress-filled life. But during his enforced bed rest he had time to reevaluate his life. He changed his work habits and later spent many happy years with his wife and children. His life became a living statement to our entire family how God used a heart attack (that He didn't send) for good.

And then there are times when He uses sickness to usher His children into His presence. Yes, Satan can use sickness and sorrow to try to destroy God's people, but God takes it, turns it around, and uses it for good. Nothing is wasted in your life! I realize there isn't any satisfactory answer to the pain and suffering your father is experiencing now. After several years of sickness, author Elizabeth Goudge said, "How an individual takes their pain, what they allow it to do to them and through them, is much more important than the pain itself."[1]

I want you to know I hurt with your entire family as you go through this time of anguish. It's difficult to see someone so dear suffer as he tosses and turns through sleepless nights, growing weaker each day in the weary work of being sick. You can be absolutely certain that this disease causing your father's body to waste away can never touch his eternal soul. In spite of the seemingly hopeless process of dying, remember that seed of eternity God planted in your dad's heart. Deep in his spirit your father knows that a life of indescribable splendor is nearer with each weary breath. God is comforting your father in ways you cannot see. As death approaches, He gives a deep, quiet peace and holds him close in His everlasting arms of love.

In the meantime, help your father understand he's not alone. Remember, Jesus also walked the long road of sorrow, suffering, and death to the cross. Jesus' death and resurrection have always been inseparable in this fallen, sinful world. Encourage your father to let Jesus restore his soul through the daily reading of the Scriptures. Be faithful in your prayers for him and encourage other family members and your small-group members to do the same. Read each card and note to him and thank God for the loving support of your church family. All the love given by family and friends is helping your dad experience God's love. I join you in giving thanks for that.

Never forget that I'm praying that you will be covered with God's blanket of comfort and reassurance. May you sense His gentle touch of love and hear His quiet whisper of peace.

Yours from the Other Side

&

Dear Child of God,

I was pleased to learn you and your mother found some consolation in my last letter. I join you in giving thankful praise to God for that. It was good to hear about the special day you and your father had yesterday. Thank you for sharing it with me. In the future I know you will treasure those precious moments of reminiscing together.

I enjoyed hearing how, as a little child, you ran to the corner to meet your father's bus at the end of each day. He scooped you up in his arms, swung you around, and carried you home on his shoulders. I can imagine the happy smiles of the people on the bus as they watched this nightly ritual. When you got home, he set you down on the porch, reached into his pocket, and pulled out a stick of gum. You always received it with great surprise, as though he were presenting you with a delightful secret. I know how special this memory is to you, and I also know the deep joy you gave to your father in return.

He instilled in you a desire for reading good books that will last a lifetime. I thought it remarkable that when you were only twelve, he began to give you books containing the life stories of some of God's special ambassadors. Your first book, *The Splendor of God*, tells the life story of Adoniram Judson, pioneer missionary to Burma, and has remained a favorite. This was followed by William Carey's story of India. Hudson Taylor, who founded the China Inland Mission, taught you lessons in prayer that you've never forgotten. But perhaps the one you like best of all is *George Müller of Bristol*, about that great man of faith. I understand you've reread that book often throughout your life. From him you learned that faith is obedience, not confidence, an excellent statement to live by. I couldn't help thinking what a priceless legacy your father gave you as a young child. I'm glad you were able to thank him, and I'm especially happy that just yesterday he was able to share with you many of the adventures he had as a boy growing up in the vast wilderness of Montana. Sometimes parents forget how interested their children are in hearing about them when they were young.

But the crowning moment of your evening together occurred as you were about to leave. When you prayed for your father, a sudden stillness seemed to permeate the room, and it was bathed in a golden light of radiant glory. You said your father felt a gentle hand on his shoulder that touched him with warmth and comfort. Time stood still, and all was steeped in peace. You both knew it was the presence of the Lord. When the moment of glory was over, you were left with an overwhelming sense of joy and wonder. I believe it was God's quiet benediction on your father's life. How fortunate you are to experience this. God chooses to work differently in each situation. Sometimes He manifests His presence just before a death and other times He's silent. In either case He's there, and He knows the physical and emotional pain experienced. He knows and He cares.

After sharing that moment together, you went home with more questions than ever about death: *What happens at death? Will he go to heaven right away? How long will it take him to get there? Will he be lonely there at first? What will he be like?* You said you were thankful for these letters because they've answered so many of your questions. I'm glad you've found comfort in reading through them again.

Having questions at this time is natural—especially after you experience a touch of eternity as you and your father did. You came up with a very intriguing portrayal of death. You said the body is like a glove and the spirit is like a hand. As long as the hand is in the glove, it can do all kinds of creative things: grip a bat, hold a shovel, steer a car, hold a ski pole, play a game of golf. But as soon as the hand is removed, all that remains is an empty glove. Each finger of the glove is still in place, yet it lies where it was tossed, vacant and hollow. The life that filled the glove is gone.

When you die, life leaves your physical body empty, like the glove. But the good news of the Bible is that your spirit goes instantly to be with the Lord.[2] As Jesus told the thief on the cross, "*Today* you will be with me in paradise" (emphasis added).[3] Elizabeth Goudge said death is like taking off your body much like you do an old coat. When you do so, you go through the door of death to another world. There's no delay. And Jesus is the door that leads from death into life.

Remember the story *Alice in Wonderland?* If she wanted to enter the enchanted world she first had to pass through the Little Door. And so it is with everyone on earth. You must pass through the little door of death if you're going to enter the big door to God's heaven. And this door is in the shape of a cross. It's the only door that leads to eternal life—the door between death and life. Death has been referred to as a "doorway to glory."[4] I like that description. If you knew the magnificent splendor waiting for you here, you'd understand why that's one of my favorite definitions of death. For all believers—including your father—death is indeed a doorway to glory. It's like going through a door into another room and discovering a welcome-home party in your honor. All of your loved ones who know Christ and have gone on ahead are there to greet you with happy shouts of joyous laughter. They can't wait to take you on a sightseeing tour of heaven.

You're fortunate to know without a doubt that your father will be in heaven. So many struggle with uncertainty over the eternal home of their parents or other loved ones. Perhaps it would be a consolation to those who wonder to know that while on earth you really don't know what goes on in the mind and heart of a person just a heartbeat away from death. But God knows. And He can be trusted to give all who *will* believe the opportunity *to* believe.

Be assured. Death for believers is a glorious homecoming, where you see Jesus face to face and hear His happy words of welcome: "Well done, good and faithful servant! Come and share your master's happiness."[5]

Yours from the Other Side

&

Dear Child of God,

Today we welcomed your father into heaven! I wish you could have seen his look of wonder and joy. Still, I know how deeply grieved you and your mother are at this time. I especially understand the heartbreak your mother is experiencing at the deep loss of being separated from her beloved husband. Death seems so final from your perspective on earth. It's often thought of as the final good-bye. It leaves a vacant place in your heart that can never be filled until you're once again reunited in heaven — a place where the word *good-bye* is never spoken. Instead only joyful *hellos* are heard. Even as we celebrate your dad's arrival here, be assured of my understanding of your deep grief over the temporary separation.

This sorrow over the separation from loved ones is the sting of death that Paul often referred to.[6] God knows it's impossible for you to see beyond the veil that separates heaven from earth. He understands the desperate longing for the one who is gone. He grieves with you over this sorrowful parting. Jesus demonstrated this grief at the tomb of his good friend Lazarus when He wept.[7] The God of all creation was showing you that it's all right to weep over the death of a loved one. In fact, it's necessary to grieve with tears. God gave them to you to bring release and healing. If you and your mother don't allow yourselves to really grieve, complete with tears, you won't be able to receive God's gentle healing. Isn't it great to know that someday at the entrance to heaven, God Himself will wipe away every tear from your eyes?[8] As humans we weep because we long to be with those we have lost to death. But would we ever wish them back?

Have you wondered why Jesus wept at the tomb of Lazarus? You remember, Lazarus had been in the tomb for four days. Where do you think the real Lazarus was during that time? In heaven. Can you imagine how he must have felt when he heard Christ's voice calling him back to earth? No one who has experienced the joys and wonders of heaven would ever wish to return to earth again. At the time Lazarus heard Jesus' voice calling him back perhaps he was sitting on a bench by the River of Life, visiting with his new friend, John the Baptist. Or he may have been before the throne of God, praising Him for the gift of salvation.

Can you imagine Lazarus's shock at hearing his Savior shout, "Lazarus! Come out!" I'm sure Lazarus must have thought, *No, Lord, please not me. I just got here!* I have to confess, I'd have felt the same way. I find myself being very thankful that I was asked to write letters to you about heaven instead of returning to earth and sharing with you personally.

Dear Lazarus, what could he do but leave the beautiful garden by the River of Life, leave John in the midst of their conversation, enter the smelly tomb, get back into the tangled grave clothes, and stumble out into the blazing Galilean sun? Now he understood for the first time something of what Jesus went through when He left the glory of heaven, "set aside the privileges of deity, and took on the status of a slave, became *human*!"⁹

No wonder Jesus wept. He knew what He was calling Lazarus back from and what He was calling him to . . . and He wept. He knew how reluctant Lazarus was to come back . . . and He wept. Jesus knew the sacrifice He was asking Lazarus to make in leaving the wonders of heaven in exchange for living once again in a rebellious sin-ridden world . . . and He wept.

For the first time, Lazarus caught a glimpse into God's amazing love. He finally understood what depths of love it took for God to come to earth and live as a human, sharing God's love with people. Oh! What a wonder!

There will be times in the days ahead when you'd like to have your father back. You'll long to have him there to fill the aching loneliness caused by his death. If he could talk to you now he might use the words of a songwriter:

> If you could see me now
> I'm walking streets of gold
> If you could see me now
> I'm standing tall and whole
> If you could see me now
> You'd know I've seen His face
> If you could see me now
> You'd know the pain is erased
> You wouldn't want me
> To ever leave this perfect place
> If you could only see me now[10]

Yes, if you could see heaven for even one moment, you would understand and never ask your father to return.

If only I could help you understand how close heaven is and how near your loved one is. Do you realize that all Jesus had to do was call Lazarus's name and he was instantly there? Because you're a prisoner bound by space and time, this is nearly impossible to comprehend. But from where I am, it's no problem at all. Someday, all of these things will be made plain to you. In the meantime, be assured that it's all right to hurt. Remember that you don't need to grieve like those who have no hope. You have the blessed hope of eternal life through Jesus Christ our Lord. May this truth be your comfort.

Yours from the Other Side

❧

Dear Child of God,

Now that your father is here, I'm sure your longing to see heaven is greater than ever. Let me try to give you a sense of what he's experiencing. Take a deep breath and imagine.

I want you to stand for a moment on the border of heaven and catch a golden beam of God's light, breathe in the warm fragrance of the flowers as they sway in the summer breeze, and let the quiet peace of God's eternal love cover you with a transparent cloud of glory. Take some time to rest in the holy atmosphere of His presence. Meditate on the truth that today the Lord is your shepherd. He promised that today you shall not want. Let Him lead you beside still waters and restore your soul, bruised and broken as you've walked through the valley of the shadow of death. Let Jesus anoint your head with the oil of blessing. May you be renewed from within as His goodness and mercy follow you today and throughout all the days of your life. Rejoice in the absolute assurance that someday you'll dwell in the house of the Lord forever.[11]

This is God's good news for you. Receive it into every part of your being. Sometimes after coming through the dark tunnels of death, it's good to take time to be quiet before the Lord. Let Him breathe on you the Breath of Life as you receive the healing touch of His comfort. It helps to go over some of the truths God has given you in the past to strengthen you, and to set your feet, once again, upon the solid Rock of Jesus Christ.

Today I thought you'd like to read what some of the saints have had to say about heaven. I think you'll find their words encouraging.[12]

- ◆ D. L. Moody, the shoe salesman who became an evangelist and founder of the Moody Bible Institute, said at his death, "This is my triumph: This is my coronation day!"

- ◆ Just before that great Bible teacher F. B. Meyer died, he wrote to his friend saying, "I have received my invitation to heaven. I am just off—see you there! Love, F. B. Meyer."

- ◆ Moments before Dietrich Bonhoffer, the brilliant German pastor and writer, was executed at the end of World War II, he sent this message to his friend: "This is the end—but for me it is the beginning!"

- ◆ Note what Lord Baden-Powell, former dean of Westminster Abbey, had carved on his tombstone: "I have gone Home!" It's as simple and profound as that.

- ◆ Joseph Bayly, an author who saw three of his sons die, was able to say of death, "Death is the great adventure beside which moon landings and space trips pale into insignificance."

- ◆ Evangelist Billy Graham said death is simply a "step on the pathway to heaven."

- ◆ John Milton described death by saying, "Death is the golden key that opens the palace of eternity."

Don't you see? For the Christian, death is simply the gateway to heaven. I know you'll find these quotations a comfort and blessing at this time in your life. There are many more quotes I could have shared with you, but I thought someday you might enjoy looking them up on your own.

Always remember that when your father celebrated his coronation day in heaven, he was welcomed home by Jesus. The angels greeted him with rejoicing as they lifted their voices in exultant praise to the King of kings and Lord of lords. Your father carried his personal gold-engraved invitation to heaven, signed with the blood of Jesus. It was then that your father made the one discovery everyone makes when they first arrive here: Besides yourself, the only thing you bring to heaven is God's eternal love for you and your eternal love for Him.

May the wonder of this truth be your comfort as you complete your journey on earth.

Yours from the Other Side

CHAPTER NINE
Reasons to Believe

Dear Child of God,

Did you ever stop to think that each time you write the date on a letter or sign an important dated document you bear witness to the life of Jesus? All of history is dated B.C. (before Christ) or A.D. (*anno Domini* or in the year of the Lord). It's remarkable to think that for two thousand years the recognized international dating system has been based on the life and death of Jesus Christ. How could the life of a simple carpenter who never wrote a book and who died the death of a common criminal change the entire course of human history? What possible answer could be given for this miraculous, historical fact of life?

The resurrection of Jesus Christ is the turning point of all history. It's an actual event that took place in space, time, and history — the cornerstone of the Christian faith. And with it came the demise of death! The bodily resurrection of Jesus is God's triumphant call of salvation to a lost and dying world. It's the message of eternal life to all who receive it.

The Resurrection is not some fictitious idea proposed by a few fishermen. It's a historical fact — truth. Jesus walked through the veil of death and back again to demonstrate for all time and eternity that death is not the final experience — life after death is. The resurrection of Jesus is the most powerful, compelling evidence we have of this almost universal belief in life after death.

Jesus not only walked bodily out of that Palestinian tomb, He deliberately chose to walk among His followers for several weeks to make sure they recognized the genuine reality of the miracle of the Resurrection. This was imperative because without the Resurrection, the Christian faith is empty and meaningless. Without it Jesus becomes merely a good teacher or example as many modern doubters are willing to propose. But Jesus made absolutely certain this option was not left open to anyone. His claims of deity leave no room for that. Read through the Gospels and see the preposterous claims Jesus made about Himself—preposterous only if they're not true. No one else has ever dared to make claims like His. Here are just a few of them.[1]

- ◆ I am the bread of life.
- ◆ I am the light of the world.
- ◆ Before Abraham was born, I am!
- ◆ I am the good shepherd.
- ◆ I and the Father are one.
- ◆ I am the resurrection and the life.
- ◆ I am the way, the truth, and the life.

No, Jesus didn't give anyone the option of thinking He was a good teacher or example without accepting Him and all of His teachings as true. Either what He said was the absolute truth or He was the world's greatest liar and deceiver—one who knowingly led people to destructive delusion.

Those who saw Jesus after His resurrection also talked with Him, touched Him, ate with Him, and staked their entire lives on the authenticity of the Resurrection. His disciples spent the rest of their lives preaching the gospel of Jesus Christ. They were absolutely convinced that Jesus had died and was now alive. Because of the Resurrection the disciples knew without a doubt who Jesus really was. They caught a vision of the splendor of God and the glory of the world to come. And because of this tenacious, unwavering certainty they were brutally tortured and died ignominious deaths, still refusing to deny the bodily resurrection of Jesus. Why? Because they knew Jesus was exactly who He claimed to be: Immanuel, God with us. Within a few years of their deaths Christianity swept through the entire Roman Empire and beyond.

Jesus' resurrection guarantees life beyond the grave for all who trust Him as Savior. Your Bible Study group asked a common question when they wondered why Jesus used the word *sleep* when He referred to death.[2] I agree that for those of you still on earth *sleep* does seem like a strange word to use in this regard. Jesus often used an unexpected word or story to jar the minds of His listeners awake. In this case He used the word *sleep* in the context of death because sleep is a temporary state of being. Sleep always ends when you wake up. As far as Jesus is concerned, death, like sleep, is temporary. As a believer when you die, you wake up in heaven. Your last breath on earth is your first breath in heaven. It's like the song "Finally Home" you've been singing since your father's death:

But just think of stepping on shore
And finding it heaven!
Of touching a hand and finding it God's!
Of breathing new air
And finding it celestial!
Of waking up in glory
And finding it home![3]

What a song! Someday you'll know from experience how true those beautiful words are.

Now don't you see why Jesus referred to death as sleep? It's like saying "good night" one moment and "good morning" the next. Jesus referred to death as sleep because both are temporary. The people laughed when He said it; they had no understanding of what He meant. They couldn't believe a grown man would walk around saying a dead person was only asleep. Still, Jesus continued to treat the dead as though they were merely sleeping. To the widow's dead son, He simply said, "Young man, I say to you, get up!" To Jairus's little daughter who had died, He said, "Little girl, I say to you, get up!" And to Lazarus, who had been dead for four days, He simply commanded, "Lazarus, come out!"[4] All three deceased people responded to the same voice that called all creation into being. And it will be the same electrifying, authoritative voice of *life* that will call forth His beloved children from the four corners of the earth at the time of the Second Coming. What an event that will be!

The only thing to add to these accounts are the words of the angel sitting atop a huge rock at Christ's empty tomb,

"Why do you look for the living among the dead? He is not here; he has risen!"[5]

Someone once asked Billy Graham how he knew Jesus was alive. He simply said, "I know, because I talked to Him this morning!"

And I know He's alive because I saw Him today.

Yours from the Other Side

❧

Dear Child of God,

Thank you for updating me on your small-group Bible study. It's been good to follow your progress through these letters. I knew what you meant when you said you've become so much closer through your weekly time of study and prayer. How could it be otherwise? As I've said before, what you're experiencing is just a tiny foretaste of what it's like with the family of God here in heaven. We often get together and talk about the greatness and wonder of our Lord Jesus Christ. We recall things we learned about Him while on earth and compare it with all we know about Him now. What a vast difference there is! I'm glad your study on heaven is going so well. For some reason, it's often a neglected subject. Yet it's one of such vitality and joy. I knew your study of heaven would be a great blessing to all of you.

You asked me to give you some specific reasons to believe in heaven that would be helpful to share with your own children as well as those taught by the young man in your group. Since this is such an important question, this letter will be a bit longer than most. As you draw to the conclusion of your study (and these letters), I'm cheering you on.

Actually that's one of the main reasons to believe in heaven. You see, I'm not the only one shouting encouragement. Remember how the writer of Hebrews spoke of a "great cloud of witnesses" affirming you throughout life's journey?[6] Take a moment to picture the saints of heaven in a grandstand filled to capacity, enthusiastically cheering like spectators at the Olympic Games. I'm sure you sensed their cheers as your group met last night with open Bibles and open hearts. Each one of you came seeking God's answers to your questions about heaven. Did you hear those witnesses shouting, "Way to go!" (No doubt your father was the loudest of all.)

The artist Raphael understood this concept of the "great cloud of witnesses." Next time you go to the art museum, note the way he depicted it in his work. When you look closely at the clouds or shining mist in the background of many of his paintings, you can often see the smiling faces of angels.

Heaven is always very close to you. Remember my earlier letter when I mentioned the thin veil that separates heaven and earth and how the angels move freely between the two? The Lord knows how hard and perilous life on earth can be. To help you along the way He has appointed certain angels to care especially for you. Sometimes you refer to them as your guardian angels.[7] Since they are never far from you, they've been involved in your life in various ways and often reach out and protect you—sometimes miraculously. Do you remember the time you were driving on an icy highway and lost control on the bridge and could never figure out how you avoided an accident? Well, that was one of many times a guardian angel intervened. God sends His angels to minister to you in countless ways. They open your eyes to sudden danger and help you in your physical weakness. They encourage you and minister to you in times of distress and need. They protect you in ways you will never be aware of until you arrive here in heaven. Then you'll look back on your days on earth and be surprised how many times God sent His angels to help you. Angels are God's messengers and are responsible only to Him. They're under His direct orders, and someday they will joyously welcome you home.[8]

The next time your group meets, why not take time for each person to share an experience when God may have sent an angel for help or protection. These kinds of conversations have a way of influencing the way you live out your faith in daily life. You find yourself becoming more aware of God's loving presence each moment. Pastor Richard Baxter put it this way, "Let your life on earth be a conversation in heaven." And that's what happens up here!

Occasionally the thin veil that separates you from heaven is drawn back and you get just a peek of what it is like. It's almost as if you are standing on the very border of heaven.

You mentioned you felt that way the day after the group met in your home. You were reading the Bible and praying at the time when suddenly you felt the loving, powerful presence of Jesus filling the room. You had to stop in the middle of your prayer and look up to see if He was actually standing there. What a moment of joyful worship that was. As wonderful as it was, it was only a touch of the glory that is waiting for you here. God permitted a tiny glimpse of heaven into your living room that day.

That reminded me of a special experience I had on earth. It was a summer evening and I was attending an open tent meeting with several hundred Christians. We were singing, "Turn Your Eyes Upon Jesus," and when I came to the part "look full in His wonderful face," I couldn't finish the song. In an instant, it seemed as if Jesus were walking toward me through a field of gently swaying wildflowers. As I looked at Him in wonder, I saw Him looking directly at me. There was an infectious twinkle of love in His eyes, and a feeling of holy awe swept over me. It happened so quickly, but it seemed as though all time stood still in silence. It was as if I stood at the edge of heaven, and eternity was etched on my heart. My life was never the same because I realized for the first time how close heaven really is. Augustine once said that heaven and earth actually "coexist side by side."[9]

The prophet Elijah experienced this same truth when he rode to heaven in a chariot of fire. (Awesome!) He left his coat or mantle for Elisha, which became a symbol for Elisha to carry on his work.[10]

The prophet Elisha recognized how close heaven really is when an army of enemies had surrounded the city of Dothan. Elisha's servant was filled with fear and Elisha prayed, asking God to open the servant's eyes. Instantly the servant saw an entire hillside filled with horses and chariots of fire—God's heavenly army![11] The horses and chariots were there *already,* but the servant didn't see them until God opened his eyes.

Enoch also experienced the closeness of heaven. He came to heaven without dying. The Bible says, "Enoch walked with God and he was no more."[12]

I mentioned Moses and Elijah on the Mount of Transfiguration in a previous letter. They were sent down from heaven to pray with Jesus shortly before His death.[13]

There's hardly a person who doesn't know about the angel of the Lord who appeared to Mary and Joseph to tell them of the Savior's approaching birth or about the angels who announced the coming of Jesus to the shepherds. They came with sky-splitting splendor, and the glory of the Lord was revealed all around them. They were joined by "the heavenly host praising God and saying, 'Glory to God in the highest!'"[14]

When Jesus was taken prisoner in the garden, He told His frightened disciples He could pray and immediately God would send sixty thousand angels to rescue Him. That's how close heaven really is![15]

Stephen stood on the edge of heaven the day he brought a brilliant, scathing message to the religious leaders in Jerusalem. They were so angry with him that they ordered him to be stoned. As he was dying, and in spite of the excruciating pain, his eyes were opened and he caught such a glimpse of heaven's dazzling radiance that his face lit up like the face of an angel, bathed in golden glory.[16]

I understand why you shake your head in wonder when you think about these things. I used to feel the same way. On earth no finite mind can ever grasp the infinite possibilities of this heavenly concept. To increase your understanding of how close heaven really is I could use an illustration, but please remember, it's imperfect and hardly compares with the vastness of this truth. As you sit in your family room with your television turned off, you don't hear any electronic sound waves or see any images of people. But with a flick of a button, there they are! How did they get there? Where are these images when the set is turned off? All you did was push the remote—an easy and uncomplicated motion—yet sound and pictures appeared. That's because they're always there—in your room—all the time. Could it be that heaven and all that is in it is as close as those unseen images? What a wondrous concept to ponder.

As your group meets and grapples with heavenly issues, it may help to consider these side-by-side questions.

1. How does the cloud of witnesses in heaven know when to encourage you as you journey through life? (How does e-mail work?)

2. How can an angel be there instantly to help you when they live in heaven? (How can you fax a letter that arrives on the other side of the world within minutes?)

3. How can you be with the Lord in a twinkling of an eye when you die? (How do your television, radio, and electricity *really* work?)

Another reason for believing in heaven is the expression of God's creativity in all aspects of the world you live in. C. S. Lewis refers to this as "the weight of glory." Some are natural wonders and some are supernatural. But all are wonders that bear witness to the God of the Bible. This is the wonder-working, creative, supernatural God who is the great I AM! This is the God who made everything we know in the universe — from the tiniest detail of an atom to the largest galaxy. He is the One who created you and me and "so loved the world that he gave his one and only Son, that whoever believes in him shall not perish but have eternal life."[17]

Why should your children (and anyone else) believe in heaven? Here are four good reasons to start with:

- ◆ The resurrection of Jesus
- ◆ The cloud of witnesses
- ◆ The closeness of heaven as demonstrated by angels in your own life and as recorded in the Scriptures concerning many saints of old
- ◆ The creativity of God in everything around you

Yours from the Other Side

Dear Child of God,

I knew that with several engineers and a medical technician in your group, it wouldn't be long before questions of scientific reasons to believe came up. Part of the problem your group had this week was that you were seeking to prove heaven with sterile logic, and it just can't be done. There's no way you can put heaven under a microscope and examine it.

It would be like trying to put love under a microscope and dissecting it so the results could stand up in a court of law as positive proof there is such a thing as love. You could only point to the results of love, not to love itself. I thought the conclusion the group reached at the end of the study was an honest one. You all agreed there were two things you could accept as truth.

1. *There is a God who is personal.* C. S. Lewis, the former agnostic British scholar, said two words brought him to the place of becoming a Christian. *God is.* And that is where every person must begin. If God is, then the next question is *What kind of God is He?* As you already know, the place to find out is the Bible—the inspired Word of God. The Bible teaches there is a supernatural God who moves throughout history in a mighty, supernatural way. This is truth. Everyone who has received Jesus as Savior has experienced the reality of this truth.

2. *God has prepared a place for His children called heaven.* He put a universal longing in each person's heart for this future home. This truth is also revealed in His Word. It's part of the beautiful image of God in each life. What kind of a cruel trick would God have played on humanity if heaven were nothing more than a master stroke of deception? The group reached the only conclusion they could have come to: the undeniable fact that God *is* truth. His Word is truth. Heaven, your future home, is truth.

I especially like the way you summed up the word *truth*. You're right, it can be a confusing subject. Yet, God's truth is the very center of the foundation of the universe. Truth can never be whatever we choose to make it. Truth is truth whether a person believes it or not. Unbelief never alters it. It's a fixed absolute. As one of your engineers said, two plus two will always equal four, regardless of what anyone chooses to believe. The law of gravity is a fixed reality of the universe. If someone says, "I don't believe in the law of gravity," the validity of the law does not change. When an apple drops from a tree, it still falls to the ground, regardless of what anyone chooses to believe. There's no way you could live in a world without absolutes because the entire universe is directed and held together by the unbreakable laws of God's absolutes as recorded in Genesis 1:1. God is truth and His truth is absolute.

I know these are difficult concepts to grasp, especially through letters. Sometimes we just have to reflect on them over and over. It helps to remember that God's existence is not dependent on whether or not anyone believes in Him. God is, period. His truth is implanted in each believer. He said, "I will put my law in their minds and write it on their hearts. I will be their God, and they will be my people."[18] Think what it would be like if everyone in the world returned to the eternal truth of God. What freedom would follow! Jesus said, "Then you will know the truth, and the truth will set you free."[19]

In closing this letter I want to mention four eternal values you will find in heaven. They are:

- ◆ truth
- ◆ goodness
- ◆ beauty
- ◆ love

These qualities are the pure essence of God. And the good news is that He has placed these same values within the heart of each person. They are the values that will continue to be enhanced throughout eternity. When your life is built upon these things, you can be absolutely certain that your foundation is firmly grounded on the Rock of All Ages, Jesus Christ.

Yours from the Other Side

♂

Dear Child of God,

Thank you for sharing the conclusion your group reached about heaven this past week. You agreed that if you really believed in heaven it would impact the rest of your life. Did you hear the great cloud of witnesses cheering on that one? I was happy to hear the group took me up on the challenge to see what would happen if you started to live each day with heaven in view. Some of the stories you shared about how the lives of your group members have changed were wonderful.

Several ways an eternal perspective can affect how we approach the dailyness of living were illustrated by the nurse's story. She told how instead of just going through the routine of entering each room, giving a short greeting, dispensing medication, and hurrying to the next room, she finds herself looking forward to the possibility of sharing God's love with each patient. She's found that she can do this through simple things like a smile or just listening more closely to what a patient is saying. She senses a new quiet spirit within her and a genuine caring for each person. She has more confidence about praying with patients who ask, and her patients seem happier to see her. Even though she has always enjoyed being a nurse, she now has a greater sense of purpose and direction as a result of keeping heaven in view.

You shared how it's been such a help in dealing with your father's death to deliberately live each day with heaven in view. Even though your dad comes to mind so often throughout each day, causing a stab of loss and sorrow, when you turn your thoughts to heaven a tiny seed of indescribable joy springs up alongside the pain. I like how you and your mother often try to picture your father cheering you both on. Thanks for sharing how just yesterday you two had a good laugh over that mental picture. You also said that your whole family has been drawn closer to each other by this new idea of living on earth with an eye toward heaven. This helps you be more open about sharing your hearts with each other. When the sorrow and pain of losing a loved one slowly begin to heal, then the joy and hope of heaven can take root. That's what happened when you and your mother felt you both had started to live again. Yes, keeping heaven in view helps give hope for today and for the future.

Most of the group agreed that living this way makes a big difference in your desire to serve Jesus right where you are — whether at home, school, work, or in your neighborhood. You've noticed a continual seed of excitement as you go through each day wondering who God will bring along to share His love with. This helps you see each person as an individual somewhere along the road of faith.

Some people journeying through life are shrouded in unbelief. They live as though none of the splendor of heaven has touched their lives. Even though the golden nugget of eternity has been placed by God in their hearts, it's become tarnished by the fool's gold of materialism—buried by the desire to make more money, buy more things, and seek more personal pleasure regardless of the cost. As a result, these people have forgotten the two things that really count in life: their relationship with God and their relationships with others.

When the hope of heaven is abandoned, the common conclusion is the one reached by Siddhartha Gautama, the founder of Buddhism, who said, "Existence is the greatest of evils."[20] What a tragic, meaningless commentary on the gift of life God has given. Yet it was the only logical solution he could come to if there were no God and no heaven. Along this same vein agnostic lawyer Clarence Darrow summed up his philosophy like this, "No life is of much value and every death is but little loss."[21] This kind of futile thinking can easily produce a world bent on destruction. You see the evidence of this philosophy throughout the twentieth century. It's one of the most blood-soaked centuries in all of human history.

The contrast between the morbid, despairing thoughts of men like Siddhartha Gautama and Darrow and the dynamic, hope-filled message of the Christian faith is profound. God's remarkable message of salvation, forgiveness, and the hope of heaven is a gift of such magnitude that it will take all eternity to truly grasp its significance. Yes, the hope of heaven makes a difference. Against the backdrop of human despair, Christ's words about truth, goodness, beauty, and love are like a blazing comet from heaven sweeping into the dark, cold world. His message isn't one of unending existence or everlasting nothingness, but of everlasting *life*. When God created man and woman, He breathed into them the breath of life. At God's appointed time, Jesus entered the world in the flesh and said, "I have come that they might have life, and have it to the full." He came that we might live abundantly.[22]

Well, your group is finding just how abundant life in Christ really is—just as He said they would. You will all probably agree with C. S. Lewis who said that when you look back on history, you will find "that the Christians who did most for our present world were just those who thought most of the next."[23]

May you be one who thinks much of heaven!

Yours from the Other Side

&

Dear Child of God,

The other day I walked over to one of heaven's art galleries to see the tapestry my friend completed. I wish you could have seen it with me. (You will someday!) It's a work of great beauty and creativity and is hanging in a place of honor because it's the newest addition to the gallery. She chose to depict the story from the Bible of Jesus gathering the little children around Him to bless them. This version of the story was set in one of heaven's gardens. Rosy-cheeked children, dressed in garments of light, nestled close to Him. Jesus listened to their happy chatter with a singing heart. You could almost hear the peals of their laughter.

On the way home, I found myself thinking of you and the joy I'm having writing to you about heaven. And then another reason to believe came to mind. I realized that each life on earth is like a tapestry of the choices a person makes on his or her journey through life. The threads are woven by God with artistic precision to form a design of exquisite beauty. Brilliant colors of ruby, emerald, turquoise—and many you haven't yet seen—are joyfully woven through times of obedient happiness. The soft colors of the rainbow are added during times of serenity and contentment. And then there are the dark colors of sorrow, disappointment, and loss carefully woven through the muted colors of comfort and gentle consolation.

But above all, the one blazing color worked throughout the entire tapestry is the shining thread of our redemption in Christ. This thread is intricately woven through every experience of a believer's life. Without it, the tapestry is void of all light. With it, the power of evil that could easily dominate life's tapestry is restrained. This precious thread is the scarlet cord of the redeeming blood of Jesus Christ touching every color of the tapestry with radiant glory.

Without the finished work of Jesus on the cross, there's

no hope for salvation. No hope of forgiveness. And no hope of heaven. It's like the old hymn says, "My hope is built on nothing less than Jesus' blood and righteousness. On Christ, the solid Rock, I stand; all other ground is sinking sand."[24] What a great adventure God has waiting for you when your life is grounded on the solid Rock of Jesus Christ and His righteousness. Then He becomes the Great Weaver of the tapestry of your life, and each day you discover He is designing a pattern of incomparable beauty. When you come to heaven, He'll present your tapestry to you with great pleasure. It will adorn the walls of your heavenly home throughout eternity.

Each time you look at this treasured tapestry you'll be reminded of God's lasting love for you and find special pleasure when you see how delicately He wove into the tapestry your good times with the study group. Get ready for a happy surprise!

Yours from the Other Side

CHAPTER TEN

The Rewards of Heaven

Dear Child of God,

In many ways I've saved one of the best things about heaven to share with you for last. You'll enjoy these next two letters because they're about rewards, crowns, and treasures. Now who isn't interested in things like that?

If only you could get a sneak preview of all that's waiting for you here. Then I could help you understand something of the vast riches deposited in your name, and you'd know why I'm so excited about what I get to share in this letter. I wish I could be more precise in telling you about the rewards waiting for you, but this is definitely one area where no earthly words are available to describe the kinds of rewards God has prepared.[1] But I can tell you they're far beyond your highest expectation. And because they're from God, you won't want to miss any of them! I'll try to give you a little insight about the rewards and crowns that can be yours.

Let's start with rewards, which are different from crowns and treasures. Rewards are given according to your devotion and obedience to the Lord Jesus while you live on earth. A record is kept from the time your name is written in the Book of Life until you arrive in heaven. There is, of course, a different record for each person's life. Some people receive Jesus as Savior in the moments just before they die, others commit their lives to Him as children, and others trust Christ somewhere in between. How *long* a person serves Christ doesn't matter; the rewards are determined by how *faithful* each person was in his or her love for God, love for others, and the use of the gifts and talents God gave the person—whether it was for one day or an entire lifetime. God is interested in the heart, not in the number of days or years you live for Him.[2]

However, as magnificent as the rewards are that God has prepared for each believer, no reward in all of heaven will ever compare with the indescribable splendor of being with Jesus face to face! Can you imagine what it will be like to see His warm smile of love and to hear Him express His appreciation for all you did for Him while you lived on earth? Nothing will ever compare with hearing His words of praise, "Well done, good and faithful servant! . . . Come and share your master's happiness!"[3] This is the highest reward you'll ever receive.

God has a lot to say about rewards in the Bible—but He also speaks much about crowns. I have to be honest with you and tell you I had to smile at some of your questions because they were the same ones I used to ask when I was on earth. *What does it mean when the Bible mentions the possibility of many crowns? Does it mean you're going to spend eternity trying to balance a stack of golden crowns on your head? Or will you have a special trophy room in your beautiful home up here where all your golden crowns are on display in a tall crystal cabinet with the light of a captured star shining on them? Will you invite guests over to* ooh *and* aah *over them?*

Of course, the answer to those questions is a loud *no*. This is definitely not what Jesus has in mind when He speaks of the crowns waiting for you. The word *crown* is a symbol of the value and honor God will bestow upon you for your faithfulness to Him. An account is kept of the many different ways you serve Him throughout your days on earth. Jesus said that even a cup of cold water given in His name is recorded.[4] (Don't you find that an amazing fact?) A crown is given in special recognition for things done for God and His kingdom. This earthly word *crown* comes close to describing this symbol of high honor and dignity.

The crown also represents the distinction that comes from living for Jesus in a suffering, hurting, fallen world—in a world full of sin, greed, hate, temptation, and bloodshed. Even the angels stand in wonder when they see how faithfully God's children walked, year after year, on their journey through life. How they trusted in God's Word and shared His love with others along the way—either through word or deed. From up here, it's truly an awesome sight to behold! That's why we stand up and cheer for you when we see you living for Jesus against such insurmountable odds. These "crowns of honor" that God has set aside for you are exceedingly beautiful, and someday you'll have the joy of laying them back down at the feet of Jesus.[5]

I know it's difficult for you to imagine receiving any more from Jesus when He's already given so much. I understand you don't even want to think of receiving a crown in payment for serving Him because your service to Him and others is simply the outgrowth of your deep love for Him. Let me assure you, God knows this because He sees your heart. But you must also remember, the crowns are significant to Him, and they will be to you too. You'll receive them with humble gratitude and the honor God wants you to have.

Here's a list of some of the crowns you'll receive when you stand before the King of kings:[6]

- ◆ The Crown of Righteousness for all those who long to see Jesus and watch and pray for His return
- ◆ The Crown of Life for all who love Him and are faithful in trials, persecution, and even death
- ◆ The Crown of Glory for all those who have been faithful in loving and caring for those God entrusted into their care
- ◆ The Crown of Rejoicing for those who shared the love of Jesus with others

Before I close, let me share an all too common scene in heaven. Just the other day a woman was welcomed home. Jesus greeted her with tenderness and joy and then took her on a tour of her new home. As they passed by the many awe-inspiring sights, she asked question after question about everything she saw. Then Jesus presented her with her rewards and crowns. She was filled with joy, gratitude, and reverence as she received each love-wrapped gift.

Some time later when they came to a room filled with unopened presents, she turned to Jesus and asked, "Who are these for?" With a gentle sadness, He replied, "These were planned for you. But they will never be opened because they're the rewards you would have received if you had been obedient when I asked you to save some time each day to spend with Me." The woman looked into her Savior's eyes with regret and quietly said, "Forgive me." Of course Jesus did and then He took away her sadness. And she will feel regret no more.

In your remaining time on earth take time to keep close to Jesus so you won't miss out on any of the delightful rewards and crowns of honor He has planned for you. Walk each day with Him in prayer. Spend time in His Word. Share His love with all you meet. And most of all, rejoice that your name is written in the Book of Life!

Yours from the Other Side

❧

Dear Child of God,

I know you've heard that old phrase, "You can't take it with you." But good news! In some cases, you can. The truth is, there are treasures you can deposit in heaven while you live on earth. Does that surprise you? These kinds of treasures are stored in heaven's bank where thieves can never break in and steal, moths or rust cannot destroy—where nothing can ever cause them to spoil or fade away.[7]

It's true that you can't bring money or other material possessions to heaven with you, but you can deposit the many good results your money provides each time you support your church or other ministries. You may not be able to go to some far-away mission field, but when you give your money to various missions, you enable others to share the gospel with those who are in such desperate need. Remember, no one gift is greater than another. Both the missionary who goes and the one who stays home, prays, and gives faithful support share equally in the treasures of heaven.

Each time you give money to feed the poor or send relief to refugees or disaster victims, each time you give your time or encouragement, you are making priceless deposits into your heavenly account. You send them up each time you share the message of salvation and forgiveness with others, when you bring mercy and comfort to those lying on beds of pain or those who are lonely, when you teach a Sunday school class or lead a congregation in worship through your gift of singing in the choir or playing an instrument. There's the treasure given for hospitality when you open your heart and home to others. Sometimes you simply share a cup of tea and a cookie with one of God's precious seniors. That, too, contributes to your heavenly account.

Be prepared for a happy surprise when you see the results of your faithful prayers for others through the years. Someday you will see the glorious results of your prayers (past and future) for your children, grandchildren, spouse, parents, friends, and others.

Can you imagine your joy in seeing the results of each prayer you uttered in Jesus' name? You will run into people here from the many mission fields you cared enough to support with your gifts of love and prayers. You'll listen to their stories of all God accomplished as He ministered to them through you.

You'll meet the surgeon you read about in the newspaper last week and prayed for as he operated on a little girl and saved her life. I thought you'd like to know she's going to be used in the years ahead in a great way to bring God's message of love to hurting people. Your fervent prayers for both the doctor and the little girl have been deposited in your account up here as part of your heavenly treasure—and don't doubt the treasure it will be to sit down and listen to their thrilling stories about how God used them for His honor and glory there on earth.

And you'll meet the nurse you saw recently on the news sitting by the bedside of a young man who was dying with AIDS. You prayed God would give her an opportunity to share the love of Jesus with her patient. She did, and he responded. He was born into the family of God shortly before he arrived here. These prayers all contribute to what God has stored in heaven for you. (By the way, I'm so glad you've discovered the importance of making the newspaper part of your daily prayers—what incredible need you find on each page. Think what would happen if Christians around the world prayed through their newspapers!)

Do you see how every kind word, unselfish act, or quiet prayer becomes a treasure of eternal value and beauty here in heaven?

By far your greatest treasure will be when Jesus takes you by the hand and you walk together through heaven's grandeur as He brings you to each person who has come to heaven because you shared the gospel with him or her on earth. Think what a joyous occasion that will be! Can you hear the happy shouts of thanksgiving? Think of the stories they'll share with you of their personal journey with Jesus. Not only will you meet them, but you'll meet their spiritual children and grandchildren who met Jesus because you shared the gospel.

And then there will be the other people you ministered God's love to in countless quiet ways. God notes them all.

The following is a little poem God used to speak to my heart when I lived on earth.

> When I enter that Beautiful City,
> And the saints all around me appear,
> I want to hear somebody tell me,
> Oh! It was you who invited me here![8]

This is your treasure.

Yours from the Other Side

CHAPTER 11

The Homecoming

Dear Child of God,

Well, the time has come, and this will be my last letter to you. Thank you again for telling me how much they have helped and encouraged you. I'll miss writing, but you know I'll be one of the first to welcome you *home!*

That brings me to your question: *What will my heavenly homecoming be like?* Again, I'll try my best to answer, but I wish I could use heavenly language.

Remember when your son returned from college for Christmas vacation? You had his room ready and waiting. The refrigerator and pantry were stocked with every snack his heart could desire. Delicious aromas of a promised favorite dinner drifted temptingly through the house. Fresh holly and candles adorned the table set with your finest crystal and china. You did all this to remind him that he's special. Burning logs in the fireplace snapped cheerily, bathing the room in warmth and welcome. Twinkling lights danced on the tree, touching everything with magic. Christmas music filled the house with gladness. Outside the stars burned frostily in the cold winter sky, and the branches on the surrounding trees seemed to be strung with diamonds as the glow from the Christmas lights kissed the gently falling snow.

Suddenly the moment of joyful anticipation arrived. The horn from your son's car blared down the street and into the driveway. As he dashed up the front steps, he tossed his hat in the air and shouted, "I'm home!" The entire family made a mad scramble to get to the door at the same time. There were open arms, warm hugs, and joyful shouts of "Welcome home!"

Now that's a homecoming!

What will your homecoming be like? Remember the time you went to the hospital for orthopedic surgery? There were anxious days of pain, tasteless food, bare walls, I.V. tubes, medication, and tedious (and sometimes painful) physical therapy. The nights were filled with loneliness, discomfort, and broken sleep. Then at last it was time to be discharged. How *good* it was to be home with all your family around you. You had your own bed with the quilt your grandmother made for your wedding gift. You had your own pillow! There were pictures on the wall and cozy lamps sending forth a warm glow of quiet beauty. A new singing filled your heart as you joyfully sighed over and over again, "Oh, I'm home!"

Now that's a homecoming!

What will your homecoming be like? Remember your college reunion? Even though you hadn't seen some of your friends for years, each person still held a special place in your heart—especially those who shared your faith in Christ. When you checked into the hotel, the lobby was bursting with one loud, happy welcome after the other. For over an hour, bear hugs were given out, accompanied by infectious laughter and joyful tears. You and your fellow believers all found yourselves agreeing, "This must be what heaven will be like!"

Now that's a homecoming!

What will your homecoming be like? Take those moments of happiness and multiply them by ten thousand times ten thousand and you'll have only a glimmer of the joyful homecoming Jesus has prepared for you. All your family and friends who know Jesus as Savior and have arrived before you will greet you with ecstatic cries of welcome and warm, loving hugs. But the supreme moment of all will be when Jesus Himself triumphantly welcomes you *home* with outstretched hands of love—the same hands that were nailed to the cross for you so long ago. He'll meet you at the gate and call you by name, receiving you joyfully into the wonders of heaven. The celestial chorus will surround you with hymns of exultation, and you will at last experience all of heaven's marvels. Heaven is filled with the joy of the Lord. As C. S. Lewis liked to say, "Joy is the serious business of heaven!"[1]

Even though you let your imagination soar above the clouds, you'll never be able to imagine the joy waiting for you at your homecoming. The Bible says, "No eye has seen, no ear has heard, no mind has conceived, what God has prepared for those who love him."[2]

Helmut Thielicke once said, "There is a homecoming for us all—because there is a Home!"[3] And what a home it is! All the years on earth are simply a prelude to the glorious symphony that follows. Lewis referred to life on earth as the title page and preface of a book. The story begins with chapter one in heaven. Are you ready for the first chapter?

I saw the Holy City . . . prepared as a bride beautifully dressed for her husband. And I heard a loud voice from the throne saying, "Now the dwelling of God is with men, and he will live with them. They will be his people, and God himself will be with them and be their God. He will wipe every tear from their eyes. There will be no more death or mourning or crying or pain, for the old order of things has passed away. . . . I am making everything new."[4]

Now that's a homecoming!

Until we meet at Jesus' feet.

Yours from the Other Side

Notes

Introduction

1. Peter Kreeft, *Everything You Ever Wanted to Know About Heaven* (San Francisco: Ignatius Press, 1990), p. 13.
2. Paul Johnson, *A Quest for God: A Personal Pilgrimage* (New York: Harper & Collins, 1996), p. 3.
3. Kreeft, p. 19.
4. Joni Eareckson Tada, *Heaven—Your Real Home* (Grand Rapids, MI: Zondervan, 1995), p. 122.
5. See John 14:1-3,9-11; Acts 1:9-11; 10:39-41; 2 Corinthians 5:21; 1 Corinthians 15:3-7,20-22; 1 Peter 2:24.
6. C. S. Lewis, as quoted by Wayne Martindale, Ph.D., ed., *Journey to the Celestial City* (Chicago: Moody, 1995), p. 24.
7. Dr. Marty Folsom, from a lecture on Hebrews, given at John Knox Presbyterian Church Equipping Center, Seattle, l996.
8. Revelation 4:1, MSG.

Chapter One: Is Heaven a Place?

1. Genesis 1:1.
2. John 14:1-3.
3. See Revelation 21:11.
4. See Revelation 22:2.
5. See John 4:1-4.
6. Raymond Moody, *Life After Life* (New York: Bantam, l976), p. 52.
7. Eugene Peterson, *Reversed Thunder* (San Francisco: Harper & Row, 1988), p. 169.

Chapter Two: Where Is Heaven?

1. See Luke 15:20.
2. See Revelation 21:22-23,27.
3. See Psalm 91.

4. Matthew 16:19, MSG.
5. See Luke 23:43; 1 Corinthians 15:51-52; 2 Corinthians 12:2-4.
6. Edward M. Bounds, *Heaven: A Place, a City, a Home* (Grand Rapids, MI: Baker, 1975), p. 35.
7. See Ephesians 4:10; 2 Corinthians 12:2,4 (Paul caught up); 1 Thessalonians 4:17 (we are caught up); Revelation 4:1 (John, "Come up here"); 2 Kings 2:11 (Elijah taken up); Acts 1:9 (Jesus taken up).
8. See 1 Thessalonians 4:16.
9. John 14:2-3.
10. Acts 1:9.
11. Acts 1:11, MSG.
12. Psalm 16:11.
13. 1 Peter 5:8.
14. John 17:15.

Chapter Three: What's the Way to Heaven?

1. See Exodus 20:1-17.
2. See Proverbs 7:1-3.
3. John 3:16.
4. Romans 3:23.
5. Peter Kreeft, *Heaven* (San Francisco: Ignatius Press, 1980), p. 222.
6. 1 John 1:7.
7. Revelation 3:20.
8. See Luke 10:20, 15:7-10; John 3:1-21; 1 John 3:14; Revelation 13:8, 21:27.
9. *The Riches of Bunyan* (New York: American Tract Society, 1850), p. 82.
10. Jeremiah 31:3.
11. See God's plan: John 5:24.
    God's gift: Romans 6:23.
    God's love: John 3:16.
    New creation: 2 Corinthians 5:17.
    God's family: Romans 8:15-16.
    God's child: John 1:12.
    Forgiveness: 1 John 1:7,9.
    Name in Book: Luke 10:20.

Inheritance never lost: 1 Peter 1:3-4.
Heir with Christ: Romans 8:17.
Heaven guarantee: Ephesians 1:18.
Joy: 1 John 1:1-3.
Rock: John 10:28-30; Romans 8:38-39.
12. 1 John 3:1-3.

Chapter Four: What Will We Be Like?

1. See 1 Corinthians 15:35-44.
2. Psalm 139:14.
3. 1 Corinthians 15:36-39, MSG.
4. See 1 Corinthians 15:42-43.
5. See Luke 24:13-35.
6. See John 20:19-27.
7. See Hebrews 13:8.
8. See Galatians 5:22.
9. See John 21:1-14.
10. See Matthew 17:1-8, MSG.
11. Luke 9:30.
12. Matthew 13:43.
13. Daniel 12:3.
14. See Isaiah 61:10, 2 Corinthians 5:21.
15. C. S. Lewis, *Man or Rabbit,* essay taken from *God in the Dock* (Grand Rapids, MI: Eerdmans, 1970), p. 112.
16. Matthew 10:42.
17. "Thank You." Words and music by Ray Boltz © 1988 Gaither Music Company ASCAP. All rights controlled by Gaither Copyright Management. Used by permission.
18. See Revelation 19:9.
19. See Matthew 22:30, Mark 12:25, Luke 20:35.
20. See Mark 13:27.

Chapter Five: What Will We Do?

1. Joseph Bayly, *Heaven* (Elgin, IL: David C. Cook Publishing, 1987).
2. See Genesis 1:28-30, 2:19.
3. See Genesis 3:17-19.

4. See 1 Corinthians 13:12.
5. Psalm 27:4, MSG.
6. Psalm 149:1,3, MSG.
7. Psalm 150:3-6, MSG.
8. Martindale, p. 26.
9. Revelation 5:13.
10. See Mark 10:13-16.
11. See Genesis 1:28-30.
12. See Mark 13:27, Revelation 19:9.
13. See Jonah 1:17.
14. J. I. Packer, *Knowing God* (Downers Grove, IL: InterVarsity, 1973), p. 99.
15. Genesis 1:1; see John 1:1-3, Colossians 1:1-18.
16. Psalm 93:1.
17. Packer, pp. 82-83.
18. Psalm 145:3.
19. Revelation 4:8.
20. See 1 John 3:2.
21. Psalm 16:11.

Chapter Six: Until We Get There
1. Philippians 1:23-24.
2. See Matthew 5:16.
3. C. S. Lewis, *The Weight of Glory* and other addresses (New York: Macmillan, 1949), p. 7.

Chapter Seven: Eternity in Our Hearts
1. See 1 Corinthians 13:12.
2. Eugene H. Peterson, *The Message* (Colorado Springs, CO: NavPress, 1993), p. 89.
3. Ecclesiastes 3:11.
4. Victor Hugo as quoted in John Sutherland Bonnell, *I Believe in Immortality* (New York, Nashville: Abingdon, 1959), p. 13.
5. See Psalm 139.
6. See 1 Corinthians 15:42,44.
7. Poem by Elizabeth Cheny.

Chapter Eight: The Problem of Pain and Suffering

1. Elizabeth Goudge, *Joy of the Snow* (New York: Coward, McCann & Geoghegan, 1974), p. 235.
2. See Matthew 17:2-3, 22:32; Mark 9:2-4; Luke 20:37-38; 2 Corinthians 5:1-8; Philippians 1:21-23.
3. Luke 23:43.
4. Herbert VanderLight, *Light in the Valley: A Christian View of Death and Dying* (Wheaton, IL: Victor, 1976), p. 79.
5. Matthew 25:21 (RSV), Matthew 25:23 (J.B. Phillips).
6. See 1 Corinthians 15:55.
7. See John 11:35.
8. See Revelation 21:4.
9. Philippians 2:6-8, MSG.
10. Kim Noblitt, "If You Could See Me Now." 1992 Integrity Praise Music/BMI and Hold Onto Music (adm. By Integrity's Praise! Music) all rights reserved. International copyright secured. Used by permission. c/o Integrity Music, Inc. Mobile, AL 36685.
11. See Psalm 23.
12. Ian Barclay, *Death and the Life After* (San Bernardino, CA: Here's Life, 1992), pp. 34-35.

Chapter Nine: Reasons to Believe

1. See John 6:35, 8:12, 8:58, 10:14, 10:30, 11:25, 14:6.
2. See Matthew 9:23-25.
3. L. E. Singer and Don Wyrtzen, "Finally Home." Copyright © 1971 Singsperation, Music/ASCAP. All rights reserved. Used by permission of Benson Music Group, Inc. Nashville, TN 37228.
4. See Luke 7:11-15; Mark 5:39-43; John 11:43.
5. Luke 24:5.
6. Hebrews 12:1.
7. See Hebrews 1:14, Psalm 91:11-20.
8. For more information about angels see Hope MacDonald, *When Angels Appear* (Grand Rapids, MI: Zondervan, 1982)
9. Augustine quoted in Wayne Martindale, Ph.D., ed., *Journey to the Celestial City* (Chicago: Moody, 1995), p. 37.
10. See 2 Kings 2:11.

11. See 2 Kings 6:15-17.
12. Genesis 5:24, see also Hebrews 11:5.
13. See Matthew 17:1-8.
14. Luke 2:8-15.
15. See Matthew 26:53.
16. See Acts 7:55-56.
17. John 3:16.
18. Jeremiah 31:33.
19. John 8:32.
20. Bonnell, p. 24.
21. Bonnell, p. 26.
22. See Genesis 2:7, John 10:10, Romans 6:23.
23. C. S. Lewis, *Mere Christianity* (New York: Macmillan, 1943), p. 104.
24. William B. Bradbury and Edward Mote, "My Hope Is Built," *Hymns for the Family* (Nashville: Paragon Associates, 1976), p. 92.

Chapter Ten: The Rewards of Heaven

1. See Matthew 5:11-12; Mark 10:29-30; Luke 6:22-23; Luke 18:29.
2. See Matthew 20:1-16.
3. Matthew 25:21.
4. See Matthew 10:42.
5. See Revelation 4:10.
6. See Crown of Righteousness: 2 Timothy 4:8; Crown of Life: James 1:12, Revelation 2:10; Crown of Glory: 1 Peter 5:2-4; Crown of Rejoicing: 1 Thessalonians 2:19-20.
7. See Matthew 6:19-21; 1 Peter 1:3-4.
8. Author unknown.

Chapter Eleven: The Homecoming

1. C. S. Lewis, *Letters to Malcolm: Chiefly on Prayer* (New York: Harcourt, Brace & World, 1963), pp. 92-93.
2. 1 Corinthians 2:9.
3. Helmut Thielicke, taken from *The Waiting Father* (New York: Harper & Row, 1959), p. 29.
4. Revelation 21:2-5.

Bibliography

Augustine, Saint, Bishop of Hippo. *The Confessions of Saint Augustine*. Edited by Paul Bechtel. Chicago: Moody, 1981.

Barclay, Ian. *Death and the Life After*. San Bernardino, CA: Here's Life, 1992.

Barker, Peggy. *What Happened When Grandma Died*. St. Louis: Concordia, 1984.

Bayly, Joseph. *Heaven*. Elgin, IL: David C. Cook Publishing, 1987.

Bonnell, John Sutherland. *I Believe in Immortality*. New York, Nashville: Abingdon, 1959.

Bounds, Edward M. *Heaven: A Place, a City, a Home*. Grand Rapids, MI: Baker, 1975.

Bunyan, John. *The Riches of Bunyan*. Edited by Rev. Jeremiah Chaplin. New York: American Tract Society, 1850.

Conyers, A. J. *The Eclipse of Heaven*. Downers Grove, IL: InterVarsity, 1992.

Criswell, William, and Paige Patterson. *Heaven*. Wheaton, IL: Living Books, Tyndale House Publishers, Inc., 1994.

Fiske, John. *Life Everlasting*. Cambridge, England: Houghton Mifflin, 1901.

Goudge, Elizabeth. *Joy of the Snow*. New York: Coward, McCann & Geoghegan, 1974.

Goudge, Elizabeth. *The Valley of Song*. London: University of London Press, 1951.

Graham, Billy. *Hope for the Troubled Heart*. New York: Walker and Company, 1991.

Habermas, Gary R., and J. P. Moreland. *Immortality—The Other Side of Death*. Nashville: Thomas Nelson, 1992.

Harbough, Rev. H. *Heaven, an Ernest and Scriptural Inquiry*. London: Lindsay & Blakiston, 1849.

Harris, Murray J. *From Grave to Glory*. Grand Rapids, MI: Academie Books, Zondervan, 1990.

Howatt, Reid J. *The Next Life*. New York, Chicago: Revell, 1910.

Jeffrey, Grant R. *Heaven . . . The Last Frontier*. Toronto: Frontier Research Publications, 1990.

Killen, Rev. J. M., M.A. *Our Friends in Heaven*. Philadelphia: Presbyterian Board of Publication, 1854.

Komp, Diane M., M.D. *A Window to Heaven*. Grand Rapids, MI: Zondervan, 1992.

Kreeft, Peter. *Between Heaven and Hell*. Downers Grove, IL: InterVarsity, 1982.

Kreeft, Peter. *Everything You Ever Wanted to Know About Heaven*. San Francisco: Ignatius Press, 1990.

Kreeft, Peter. *Heaven.* San Francisco: Ignatius Press, 1980.

Kreeft, Peter. *Love Is Stronger Than Death.* San Francisco: Ignatius Press, 1992.

Landis, Robert W. *The Doctrine of the Resurrection of the Body*. Philadelphia: Perkins, & Purves, 1846.

Lewis, C. S. *The Great Divorce*. New York: Macmillan, 1946.

Lewis, C. S. *A Grief Observed*. New York: Seabury Press, 1961.

Lewis, C. S. *The Joyful Christian*, New York: Collier Books, Macmillan, 1977.

Lewis, C. S. *Letters to Malcolm: Chiefly on Prayer*. New York: Harcourt, Brace & World, 1963.

Lewis, C. S. *Man or Rabbit,* essay taken from *God in the Dock*. Grand Rapids, MI: Eerdmans, 1970.

Lewis, C. S. *Mere Christianity*. New York: Collier Books, MacMillan, 1943.

Lewis, C. S. *The Screwtape Letters.* Westwood, NJ: Barbour & Co., 1990.

Lewis, C. S. *The Weight of Glory and Other Addresses*. New York: MacMillan Publishing Co., Inc., 1949.

Lucado, Max. *The Applause of Heaven*. Dallas: Word, 1990.

Martindale, Wayne, Ph.D., ed. *Journey to the Celestial City*. Chicago: Moody, 1995.

Moody, Raymond. *Life After Life*. New York: Bantam, 1976.

Nouwen, Henri J.M. *Beyond the Mirror*. New York: Crossroad Publishing, 1991.

Nystrom, Carolyn. *What Happens When We Die?* Chicago: Moody Press, 1992.

Peterson, Eugene H. *Reversed Thunder*. San Francisco: Harper & Row, 1988.

Peterson, Eugene H. *The Message*. Colorado Springs, CO: NavPress, 1993.

Springer, Rebecca. *Within Heaven's Gates*. Springdale, PA: Whitaker House, 1984.

Smyth-Paterson, J. *The Gospel of the Hereafter*. New York, Chicago: Revell, 1910.

Stowell, Joseph M. *Eternity*. Chicago: Moody Press, 1995.

Stedger, William L. *If I Had Only One Sermon to Preach on Immortality*. New York: Harper & Brothers, 1929.

Tada, Joni Eareckson. *Heaven — Your Real Home*. Grand Rapids, MI: Zondervan, 1995.

Tangvald, Christine Harder. *Someone I Love Died*. Elgin, IL: Chariot Books, David C. Cook Publishing Co., 1988.

Thielicke, Helmut. *The Waiting Father*. New York: Harper & Row, 1959.

Walker, Williston. *A History of the Christian Church*. New York: Scribner, 1959.

Winter, David. *What Happens After Death?* Oxford: A Lion Pocketbook, 1991.

VanderLight, Herbert. *Light in the Valley: A Christian View of Death and Dying*. Wheaton, IL: Victor, 1976.

About the Author

HOPE MACDONALD is a well-known speaker at retreats and churches throughout the United States and several other countries. She is the author of five books with 500,000 in print in nine languages. She and her husband, Dr. Harry MacDonald, worked for many years with the mission of Young Life. They spent six months studying with Dr. Francis Schaeffer in Switzerland and later served as missionaries in Brazil. Upon returning to the United States, Hope's husband became senior pastor of John Knox Presbyterian Church in Seattle, where they make their home.

If you liked Letters From Heaven, be sure to check out these other great titles from NavPress.

The Homesick Heart

We all have yearnings we can't articulate. This book will show you how your longings actually reflect God's own longing for you in order to bring you into close communion with Himself.

The Homesick Heart

(Jean Fleming) $8

Harsh Grief, Gentle Hope

Mary White's only son was brutally murdered in a senseless act of violence. She shares the hope she found in God in this terrible ordeal and offers compassion and hope to others facing severe loss.

Harsh Grief, Gentle Hope (Mary White) $9

Calm My Anxious Heart

You can escape worry and find true contentment. *Calm My Anxious Heart* helps women grow in contentment as they address its barriers and how to overcome them. Includes a twelve-week Bible study.

Calm My Anxious Heart (Linda Dillow) $14

Companion Journal/$10

Detours, Tow Trucks, and Angels in Disguise

Sometimes God is found where you least expect Him to be. Filled with true-to-life stories, this book will make you laugh and cry as you see God at work in your life.

Detours, Tow Trucks, and Angels in Disguise (Carol Kent) $12

Get your copies today at your local bookstore, or call (800) 366-7788 and ask for offer **#2131**.

Great studies by Cynthia Heald.

Becoming a Woman of Freedom

If you feel like your Christian life is weighing you down, this Bible study will give you a second wind. Learn to identify and lay aside those burdens that make you feel "stuck."

Becoming a Woman of Freedom
(Cynthia Heald) $7

Becoming a Woman of Prayer

God designed women to seek Him in all they do. This Bible study will encourage you to become a woman whose life is characterized by constant conversation with God.

Becoming a Woman of Prayer
(Cynthia Heald) $7

Becoming a Woman of Purpose

Do you experience success and still feel unsatisfied? This Bible study will give you a better understanding of God's purpose for your life—to love and serve Him.

Becoming a Woman of Purpose
(Cynthia Heald) $7

Becoming a Woman of Excellence

Who are you? Our best-selling Bible study helps women discover who God designed them to be, giving them the freedom to serve and please God.

Becoming a Woman of Excellence
(Cynthia Heald) $7

Get your copies today at your local bookstore, visit our website, or call (800) 366-7788 and ask for offer **#2163**.

NAVPRESS
BRINGING TRUTH TO LIFE
www.navpress.com
Prices subject to change without notice.